To Gene & Elizabeth —
Keep on dancing!
Fath. Bill Skeehan

To DANCE With A CROSS On Our BACK

Reflections on the Word Made Flesh

Father BILL SKEEHAN

To Dance With a Cross on Our Back

Published by
Meddler's Books
5500 Douglas Lane
Bartlesville, OK 74006

© 1998, Father Bill Skeehan. All rights reserved. No part of this book may be reproduced, stored in a retrieval system, or transmitted in any form or by any means, except in the case of brief quotations printed in articles or reviews, without prior permission in writing from the publisher.

Design and typesetting by Genesis Publications.

Cover design by Genesis Publications.

Printed in the United States of America.

Unless otherwise noted, Scripture references are from the New American Bible, © 1987 by Thomas Nelson, Inc., Nashville, Tennessee.

ISBN 0-9663906-0-1

*Dedicated to
the "meddlers" of the
Community of St. James,
with
special acknowledgment to
the late Anthony de Mello,
to whom I am indebted for
his collection of wise sayings*

CONTENTS

Chapter 1	SACRAMENTS	11
Chapter 2	REBIRTH	35
Chapter 3	FAITH IN CHRIST	57
Chapter 4	COMMUNITY	79
Chapter 5	BEING CHURCH	101
Chapter 6	SUFFERING	123
Chapter 7	BEATITUDES	141
Chapter 8	WITNESSING	161
Chapter 9	SPIRITUALITY	185
Chapter 10	COMPASSION	201
Chapter 11	PRAYER	219
Chapter 12	POVERTY	237

PREFACE

"We are both…doing a lot of reflecting on our lives; therefore, it seemed as though an angel had placed us there that Sunday to hear the words that you were going to offer. It was so refreshing. You touched our lives!"
—Dave & Julie, visitors to St. James, Dec. 1997

The making of this book was inevitable. For many years parishioners and visitors alike have requested copies of Father Skeehan's homilies. He has a gift that enables him to make Scripture come alive and take root in our lives. Soon the idea of a book was born—born not by Father Bill, but by those to whom he ministers. While copies of homilies eventually became easy to obtain, the agreement to publish his works in book form was much later in coming.

More than a year ago, a group of women began "meddlin'." Things soon began to fall in place and eventually Father Bill agreed to this project. We began with this mission statement:

> With the hope of inspiring all people of faith to meditate on the integral relationship between Scripture and life in this century, we have come together to compile a collection of Father Bill's writings which will reflect his Christ-inspired vision, philosophy, and personality. In doing so, may our efforts reach out, through his poetic voice, to draw our circle, our St. James family and

our extended community into deeper communion with each other, and, ultimately, with God.

With a short schedule, ambitious hands and the help of the Holy Spirit, we have reached this milestone. This book is a gift to all who want the Word to take hold of their hearts and their lives.

CIRCLE 4 MEDDLERS
THE COMMUNITY OF ST. JAMES

INTRODUCTION

For historical reasons, American Catholic Christians have a tendency to regard religion as relevant to our personal lives but not to the structures of society.

I remember some years ago a religious educator from the South stated that, where she came from, if a preacher talked about social or political issues, the congregation said, "He's quit preachin' and gone to meddlin'." So, I've gone "to meddlin'." I have been a meddler for 38 years, and the idea would look good on my tombstone: The Meddler.

A number of persons in the Community of St. James, including a group of women, can also be called "Meddlers." They have meddled and meddled to convince me to publish this work. I acquiesced reluctantly because I believe that, like the Word, homilies should be heard and not read.

The thrust of my homilies (and not all are totally original) is incarnational: that the Word take flesh and dwell in our hearts, molding and shaping us to be epiphanies of Christ in our troubled world, "meddlin'" in the economic, political and social dis-order.

If we truly attend to Jesus' be-attitudes—his way, life and truth—whether in good season or bad, the Spirit of God will enable us "to dance with the Cross on our back."

Chapter 1

SACRAMENTS

SLOW FOOD

Is fast food
really food
or just an illusion
fit for fast lane folks
symbolic of
the quick fix
or instant everything
filling the tummy
with nothingness
as we fill
our eyes and ears
with the emptiness
of artificial sound
of AM radio
and cable TV
never knowing
or evidently needing
the quiet silence
in which to be
to become
who we are
a people
kneading nourishment
the bread
of Word and Sacrament

slow food
fit for families
for emptied hearts
of servant people
meals that make
the many
to become one
through shared stories
to reveal
Real Presence
of whom we can say:
"We have met Community
and he is us."

FEAST OF CORPUS CHRISTI
1 Corinthians 11:23–26; Luke 9:11–17

The feast of Corpus Christi is a good occasion to reflect on the core meaning of the Eucharist. I say "core meaning" because during the Middle Ages when this feast first entered into the Church calendar, Christians had moved pretty far away from the core in their Christian piety. Gathering around a table to break bread and share a cup of thanksgiving had given way to stress on the food itself—the sacred host. *Venerating* the host had replaced the *sharing* of a meal. The *object* on the altar had become more significant than the action of thanksgiving that surrounded it, and the liturgy of the Mass had evolved to the point where one could easily forget that it all began with a meal around a table. People, in those times, even paid priests to hold up the host longer at the elevation in the belief that souls were being released from purgatory while the host was elevated. This kind of superstition amuses us now but we still risk the danger of dabbling in magic.

Emphasis on the *things* of the Eucharist, the bread and the wine, has for many centuries overshadowed the *action* of the Eucharist. For good or ill this is part of our heritage and it is not easy to overcome. If someone were to ask you, "What are the symbols of the Eucharist," what would you answer? In my experience most Catholics promptly answer: "Bread and wine."

Chapter 1 • Sacraments

But that's not the correct answer. The original Eucharistic symbols are not *things*; they are *actions*. The original Eucharistic symbols are *breaking* bread and *sharing* the cup. Otherwise, Paul and Luke in today's readings wouldn't make much sense. Paul is telling the Corinthians that they have forgotten their catechism. The Christians of Corinth were going through the motions of breaking bread and sharing the cup for they were split into factions. Paul's point was that they should "recognize the body"—not body of Christ *Eucharist* but body of Christ *people*. The body of Christ, Corpus Christi, is *ourselves* before it is bread and wine. We must recognize the presence of the body of Christ among us *before* we lift the bread and proclaim "the body of Christ" in communion. We are the body of Christ before we take the body of Christ. We are the body—and furthermore our celebration with the bread and cup is meaningless—in Paul's words, it brings "condemnation," unless we act like Christians and work to settle injustices and tensions in our own community.

In still another way Luke tells us that the Corpus Christi—the body of the Lord—is not a matter of objects lying on the altar. Jesus taught his disciples that an essential part of their ministry was breaking bread together. A good portion of Luke's Gospel takes place around the table…around dinners hosted by renewed people like Levi and Zacchaeus or by legalists who couldn't understand how Jesus could eat and drink with the backwash, the losers in society. When Luke comes to the Last Supper, he has already laid out the implications of what it *means* to "Do this in memory of me:" forgiveness, reconciliation, unity, harmony restored, love celebrated, commitment to caring for one another, sharing one's blessings.

The reality, the authenticity of Christ's words at the Last Supper was found in all that he had said and done—before he came together with his friends for that last meal. He *had already* been—during his public life—broken, poured out, and spent for them.

The disciples could believe that Jesus could give them his body and blood in bread and wine because the wonders of his love had been already witnessed among them. The church that is the body of Christ is called to that same authenticity. A church that dares to say "Amen" to "this is my body which is broken for you" must show in its daily life that it is a compassionate and nurturing community which in its acts of compassion and nourishment proclaims to the world that it *is* what it professes to be; namely, the Body of Christ in the world.

> WE, BUMBLING AS WE ARE, ARE NEVERTHELESS THE BODY OF JESUS CHRIST.

So the church makes the Eucharist and the Eucharist makes the church. If we are not already the body of Christ we could not say over lifeless bread, "This is my body." This is an awesome, awful, terrifying fact that must be faced: *we*, bumbling as we are, *are* nevertheless the body of Jesus Christ and that's why we can feast as we do upon that same body. Anything less than love is unworthy of us. This

Chapter 1 • Sacraments

kind of life—a life of love and forgiveness, reconciliation, commitment to others—gives a firmer "amen" because it has seen and touched the body of Christ in places and situations far removed from church buildings and acts of worship. This kind of life acknowledges that it takes from the hands of the priest or minister that which it already is.

Next Sunday we will begin to celebrate the Communion Rite under both forms: bread and wine. This is the restoration of the common practice in the early Church, a practice that came to an end around the 11th or 12th century. The emphasis had shifted: liturgy became more and more the domain of the clergy and attention was focused not on the sacramental action of eating and drinking, but rather on the objects—especially bread, which could be more easily seen and therefore reserved.

Rather than face the Protestant Reformation honestly, the Church turned to pouting—took her marbles and went home. The Council of Trent, through law, maintained the practice of bread alone against the Protestant reformers who had restored the cup. Not until Vatican II in the early sixties did the official church begin to see the need to reemphasize the sacramental action of eating and drinking.

Now the question is: Why all the big fuss? The answer is rather simple, deeply human and therefore theologically valid. In Baptism, water as an object is not significant. In Confirmation, oil as an object is not significant. In Eucharist, bread as an object is not significant. In Baptism, it is rather the *pouring* of the water—the washing, the action—that is significant.

In Confirmation, it is the *anointing* action that is significant. In Eucharist, it is the *breaking* of the bread, the *pouring* of wine, the *eating* and *drinking* together that is significant.

Nor, I might add, is the *static* presence of Jesus' body and blood significant. Each one of us has a body, has blood. You have a body, you have blood. I have a body, I have blood. So what? Did you ever try to relate with another person merely having a body and having blood? Did you ever communicate with anyone's body and blood? Ridiculous, you say? Maybe, but not for Hugh Hefner. He's made millions with the body as *object* ignoring the dignity and significance of the *person*. When Jesus took up the bread and wine at the Last Supper and said, "This is my body broken for you; this is my blood poured out for you," he was clothing and celebrating in ritual action something he had already been doing his entire public life: his *person* being broken, poured out, spent for his friends. "There is no greater love than this: to lay down, break, pour out, spend one's life for one's friends." His action at the Last Supper was a prelude to Good Friday—the finalization—the completion of many dyings in his life which bore fruit in his resurrection.

The Eucharist today is a memorial celebration of the new covenant, the new friendship, the new relationship established in Christ between God and his people. And we are those people, "dis-membered" people, hoping to be "re-membered" through his loving friendship.

We come here not to adore, not to bow and scrape, not to feel like slaves before the awesome presence of the Creator God, but rather to celebrate his love, his forgiveness, his friendship. And this celebration will have guts—significance—only to the degree to which we give *flesh* to that love, that friendship, that forgiveness in our own relationships on a day-to-day basis. Otherwise, Sunday Mass is an empty gesture, a meaningless sign. To understand that is to understand how I feel when I stand up here Sunday after Sunday and *say* those words, "This is my body broken for you" and "…my blood poured out for you," knowing in my own heart that this is not magic—no abracadabra here—but rather a command to me, in memory of Jesus, to freely and literally be broken, poured out, spent in serving you. Small wonder that some Sunday mornings I'd rather not be here.

Where else in life do we significantly celebrate friendship, if not at a meal? If you think about it, you have *never* in your entire lives celebrated any significant event with family or friends or even strangers without eating and drinking together. Never! This morning we are having a reception for our graduates. Are we going there because we need sustenance, because we are hungry? No, we are going to share food together because that's how we humans celebrate friendship: the sharing of our lives together, the sharing of our achievements together, our struggle to become whole persons—to celebrate the reality that we have been sustained, nourished, blessed because of these friendships. As bread is the staff of life, so wine is life's delight. Its presence means and brings festivity, fellowship, rejoicing in creation. In Eucharist, bread and wine—signs of Christ's personal presence—do not cease being what they humanly signify. They simply, in faith, enter into and bring about a deeper significance. By taking the cup, we express and celebrate the deepest fellowship with Christ in his death and resurrection, as well as express and celebrate our lives together—lived out in him and according to his values.

AT THIS TIME

"During the meal he took bread, blessed and broke it, and gave it to them."
—Mark 14:22–26

I, too,
am bread and wine
blessed, broken,
and poured out;
blessed in covenant:
word and sign;
broken for others
as my giftedness
(time, talent, wealth)
is given on behalf of,
freely laid down for
the Other
and the many.
What greater love is there
than to…?

Chapter 1 • Sacraments

THE BAPTISM OF THE LORD

Isaiah 42:1–4,6–7; Acts 10:34–38; Mark 1:7–11

The Pacific Northwest has just experienced the extraordinary power of water. We witnessed what the flood waters did in our community in 1986. We also helplessly watched the waters destroy communities along the Missouri and Mississippi rivers. When folks finally come out of the water, they are awed by a power over which they had little control. Water is a force so powerful that it cleanses and destroys—so is baptism. Water is also a force so powerful that it brings and restores life—so is baptism.

Oddly enough, Jesus begins his reign at the water's edge. He did this, not because he needed saving, but to *identify* himself fully with a humanity estranged from God. In the waters of his baptism, Jesus submitted himself symbolically to the last reality of being human: death…as John plunges him *under* the water. His later struggle would lead to the cross. Coming *out* of the water, Jesus was given energy and life. He was ordained, invested, celebrated as victor *over* death for us. Jesus, like the rulers of old, submitted himself to John for this royal anointing. This one, however, would not know palaces, thrones, armies.

God's saving power is focused in the person of Jesus as "Suffering Servant." Having identified himself by coming *to* the water, and submitted himself to the power of death *in* the water, Jesus came *out of* the water—ordained, chosen for a mission *against death* and *for life*.

Our lives in Christ's reign also begin at the water. We are called by the Spirit, within community, to the waters of Baptism. We come seeking life, a breath, a Spirit that we cannot make or buy for ourselves… something WalMart doesn't carry. All we have to offer is our self-centered lives that we know will end. So we come to the waters acknowledging our temporality, our limits, our death, and our inability to do anything about it. As we go to the waters of Baptism, we meet Jesus; we are joined with him and *to* his death. There in the water we begin *our* struggle with death. It is the beginning of our burial. We have been marked with the cross forever.

Coming *out* of the water we are granted a *new* life, a resurrected life, a life in the reign of God. We too are invested, ordained, celebrated as members of God's royal family.

This Kingdom is *in* the world, but not *of* it. Inhabiting it means that we are now servants *to* the world. Our mission is to be "a light to the nations," as Martin Luther King was. Our job description was written *at, in* and *out of* the water. We too are called to be suffering servants for the sake of the world. Our first priority is God and neighbor—*all* neighbors. We will bring light into the darkness of the weak, the sick, the suffering. We will speak up for those society rejects and fears. We will struggle with the oppressed; we will love the hate-mongers *out of* their self-consuming prisons:

> To our bitterest opponents we say:
> We shall match your capacity to inflict suffering by our capacity to endure suffering. Throw us

in jail, we shall still love you. Bomb our home and threaten our children, we shall still love you. Send your hooded perpetrators of violence into our community at the midnight hour and beat us and leave us half dead, and we shall still love you. Be assured that we will wear you down by our capacity to suffer. One day we shall win freedom, not only for ourselves. We shall so appeal to your heart and conscience that we shall win you in the process and our victory will be a double victory.

—Martin Luther King, Jr.

The words of the prophet will take on a new meaning for us: "Let justice roll down like waters and righteousness like an ever-flowing stream." We will comfort the grieving with nothing less than the promise of resurrection and life everlasting.

And *work* is not the operating principle in all this, rather an attitude of heart and spirit...the Beatitudes—the attitudes of Martin Luther King. This new life, lived now, means that we can go to our graves trusting not in ourselves but the God who brought us *to* the waters, who overcame our limitations and death *in* the waters, and who called us to a new and full life of service *out of* the water.

This is, of course, the real reason why we bless ourselves as we *enter* church—not out of pious sentimentality or superstition. We do it to remind ourselves, Sunday after Sunday, *who* we are; that we first entered our community of faith, the church, *through* water, signed with the Cross, anointed to witness and mission a*gainst death* and *for life*, all in the name of the Father, Son and Spirit. Amen.

WASHING FEET

John 13:1–15

Holy Thursday

A table and some chairs,
some bread and some wine,
some words of love and
some words of mystery.

And you take the bread
and you take the wine,
and then you feed us
with your life—and
isn't that enough?

Isn't that enough?

And I sit there
slowly chewing and sipping
on that haunting question,
I hear the answer, "No."

And I must know that I too
must give up my body
and give up my blood,
and have you pick me up and say,
"This is my body and
this is my blood
which will be given up
for all. Do this in
remembrance of me."

Chapter 1 • Sacraments

The poet, Andrew Costello, touches deeply the mystery of the Eucharist. In the early Christian Community the words "Body of Christ" did not refer to the Eucharist but rather to the Church itself. When this community gathered at the Eucharist out of the fullness of its own being—that is, the Church—Christ was present in the gifts of bread and wine. St. Augustine, preaching in the fifth century, told the newly baptized, "If you are the body of Christ and its members, it is *your* sacrament that reposes on the altar of the Lord. It is *your* sacrament that you receive. When you approach the table of the Lord," he told them, "you answer 'amen' to what you yourself are. *Be* then," Augustine said, "a member of the body of Christ to verify your 'amen'!" Augustine summed up the intimate relationship between the community and the Eucharist in these words: "*Be* what you *see* and *receive* what you *are!*" (Body of Christ people taking the Body of Christ Eucharist.)

This is the theology that was recovered during the days of Vatican II, long buried by the Council of Trent and the counter-reformation, still ignored by most of the hierarchy: bishops and priests. Augustine's theology is that Christ is present in the sacrament of bread and wine only *because* he is *first* present, in a most intimate way, in the whole life of the Church—his body in the world. Christ's Eucharistic presence—in turn—flows into the life of the whole body and further builds up the community of faith in what can be called Christ in the form of a community. (Note that there is little said here in relation to the individual.)

There is *nothing* in our authentic tradition that would validate a "zap"—"Hee-e-ere's Jesus!" image—as if a remote Jesus were being "beamed down" from heaven when certain words were said. Body of Christ—Corpus Christi—is the reality of God *and* humanity caught together in a communion of life through Christ. Today we reverse the gospel story. Having celebrated ourselves as Christ's body—having taken his Eucharistic presence, we "go into the city"—sent by Christ to discover there how to verify our "amen." We "go into the city" to "*wash feet,*" to give flesh to our Eucharistic meal; to be broken and poured out and spent for one another—and *all* others; to share the meal of our resources, talents and time with the poor; to be inclusive, not exclusive; to be instruments of the reign of God coming *now* and a foretaste to the external feast in the Kingdom's fullness.

> WE ARE SENT BY CHRIST…TO BE BROKEN AND POURED OUT AND SPENT FOR ONE ANOTHER.

We are not literalists. We do *not* take Scripture literally; we take it metaphorically. We are called to be poetic, to transcend the literal. "Washing feet" does not mean literally *washing feet.* It means metaphorically and in truth to be *servants* in *all* of our relationships and thereby verify our "amen."

Chapter 1 • Sacraments

THE WORD MADE FLESH

Exodus 24:3–8; Hebrews 9:11–15; Mark 14:12–16,22–26

We believe in the incredible: *the fact that the eternal Word took flesh in Jesus of Nazareth.*

We, therefore, seem to celebrate the human body endlessly. We cherish sacraments that affirm God's presence in our births and deaths, our confession of sin and the marking of commitment.

Not only do we celebrate when Jesus was born, we commemorate those precise moments when he was conceived and circumcised. And after we honor the Holy Spirit and the Trinity at this time of the church year, our rituals turn to Christ's flesh. We celebrate his *heart* as sacred, his *blood* as transfigured.

Though we are quite aware of the body's frailty and fate, its goodness remains an inescapable fact. Thomas Aquinas insisted that the body could never be the ultimate source or immediate cause of evil. Otherwise, how could the incarnation have occurred? How could Christ have been a human body? The feast of Corpus Christi has had—over the centuries—special associations, but whatever its historical genesis and development (some of it quite bizarre), the feast of the Body and Blood of Jesus has a thematic reach that touches the core meaning of our salvation and the extent of our mission.

First, it is a celebration of Jesus Christ's body—a body like our own, genetically coded, conditioned by birth, developing through life and undergoing the terrible relinquishment of death. It is a celebration of his body, moreover, which he identified with bread and wine in his Last Supper, given to us as the food of faith. We literally take into *our own* bodies the body of the Savior. This re-enacts the Incarnation: God once again takes human flesh. *We are the indwelling.* The Body of Christ Eucharist nourishes the Body of Christ people.

Communion also re-enacts our redemption. Each time we celebrate this sacrament we embody the covenant of Christ, wherein God sees *in us* the flesh of Christ. It was not by the "blood of goats and calves, but by his own blood" that our redemption was achieved, and our consciences cleansed. Jesus Christ, "body, blood, soul and divinity," becomes substantially one with *our* bodies as our very food and sustenance. Thus God *beholds* each of us and *sees* the beloved Son sent to save us.

> THE BODY AND BLOOD OF CHRIST IS NOT ONLY OUR REDEMPTION. IT IS OUR TASK.

But it is not only God's vision of us that is affected. Our own vision of ourselves and of each other is transformed. If we fully penetrate this mystery, we are empowered to see each other as God sees us: as the body and blood of Christ. The consecration at the Eucharist is marked by the words: "This is my body…This is my blood." Through our Communion, the words apply to each of us. Transubstantiation, then, applies not only to the appearances of bread and wine, it also applies to the appearances of human flesh, *our* human flesh. Perhaps this is the Eucharistic meaning of Jesus' parable of the last judgment in Matthew 25.

When all the nations of the world are gathered together, the Son of Man utters those strange words: "Insofar as you did it *to* the least of these, you have done it *to* me." In the body of the prisoner or stranger, in the body of the hungry or naked, the disconsolate or the sick, a second transubstantiation has taken place. Christ has said over the least of us: "This is my body." In his sermon "The Weight of Glory," C. S. Lewis wrote, "Next to the Blessed Sacrament itself, your neighbor is the holiest object presented to your senses." Christ's body is as hidden in the least of us as it is under the appearances of bread and wine. Both require an uncommon and daring faith. When we labor for human rights, when we shelter the poor, when we dismantle the bombs, when we protect the unborn, when we reach out to the criminal—we do these things not as political activists or social workers. We do them not as liberals or conservatives. We do them as people who worship the *incarnate* God. The body and blood of Christ is not only our redemption. It is our task.

MARRIAGE COVENANT

Genesis 2:18–24; Hebrews 2:9–12; Mark 10:2–12

Cast your bread…

They returned home, happy but tired after celebrating their 40th wedding anniversary with their children and grandchildren, loving relatives, and old friends. Before falling into bed, he offered to make a late night snack for both of them. While she slumped into a stool along the kitchen counter, he collected the ham, cheese and mustard from the refrigerator. Reaching into the bread box, he took out what turned out to be the last four slices of bread. He carefully made two sandwiches and cut each in quarters, the way she liked them. He placed one of the sandwiches on a plate and placed it in front of her.

"How come you always give me the sandwich with the heel of the bread?" she demanded to know. "Forty years we've been married and you always, always give me the heel of the bread. I know I've never said anything before, but honey, I really hate the heel of the bread. Why do you give me the heel all the time?"

Embarrassed, he just shrugged his shoulders and stammered, "I always give you the heel of the bread because it is my favorite piece."

—Connections

In Jesus' time, there was little appreciation of love and giving in marriage: marriages were always arranged in the husband's favor, the husband could divorce his wife for just about any reason, the woman was treated little better than property. But Jesus teaches that marriage is much more than a legal contract or arrangement. Marriage that is sacrament is centered in the love of God, love that knows *no* condition or limit in its ability to give and forgive—love that is realized in covenant.

Covenant is much more appropriate than talk of contracts, laws, rights and obligations. A covenant is a religious commitment involving vows or sacred promises—not just a contract. (Unless you are a celebrity or fabulously rich you don't need a lawyer to get married, only to get divorced.) Covenant describes God's relationship to us, a promise that we will be God's people and that God will be father and mother to us.

In marriage, we have a micro-covenant: two persons vow to find unity in a shared life, a new community. In their minds and bodies, they are called to be as good as God to each other.

From Genesis, in that description we heard of the first marriage, Adam is in control, speaking the words of tenderness and acceptance that we associate with nuptial love. Adam is superb and Michelangelo painted him that way. In later scenes he becomes less. We find him like a pouting child, kicking at God, passing the buck, blaming "the woman you gave me."

The myth we call Genesis simply points to the imperfections in every human relationship, and that should make us reflect on the constant need to give and receive forgiveness, or at least to live in an atmosphere of reconciliation. Michelangelo also painted the first couple as they departed paradise. *They ate together.* The solution today would be divorce.

Love evidently is more a matter of the will than emotion, of choice rather than passion. We will love someone, that is, *we make a choice,* in many instances where choices are not appealing. And we will choose to persevere in love with each other, even when we are unattractive to the other.

When I preside over a marriage rite, I do not ask, "John, do you love Susan?" I ask, "John, *will* you love Susan?" Love is defined here as something we *promise* to do—a future activity—the *result* of marriage rather than its *cause.* There are other cultures such as the Chinese or Lebanese where marriages were arranged and love came afterward. As one Chinese put it, "You westerners marry when the pot is at boil. Our marriage is like putting the pot on the fire. Before long it will come to a boil."

> LOVE IS MORE A MATTER OF THE WILL THAN EMOTION, OF CHOICE RATHER THAN PASSION.

I've told young people during the wedding rite that they were *not* getting married today; they were celebrating—stopping for a moment to shout "hooray" for their commitment, this good beginning. And down the road twenty-five or thirty or forty years they may, hopefully, be able to stop and look at each other and say, "We're married!"

Today, the interpretation of Jesus in the Gospel is a hard-line one: he is laying down the law. But I would rather put it that he is reminding us of an ideal. It is difficult to imagine that he is not compassionate with those who have to live with less than the ideal.

Chapter 1 • Sacraments

A WORD REFLECTION AT A WEDDING MASS

John and Annette, you will shortly be married,
through your own ministry
as priests of this Sacrament;
the two of you becoming one,
yet remaining yourselves.

At Communion time
you will share the Eucharist,
the give and take of nourishment
to sustain your oneness in diversity;
food that will give flesh
to your vows.

John, you will be saying to Annette:
"I am willing, like this bread,
to be broken for you."

Annette, you will be saying to John:
"I am willing, like this wine,
to be emptied for you."

Paradox: To be broken
is to become whole;
To be emptied
is to become full.

And then, if together,
out of that wholeness and fullness,
you share with all others:
the least
of Jesus' brothers and sisters,

Your marriage itself
will be a sacrament,
a daily living sign
of Christ's real presence
and his Kingdom coming
on earth
as it is in heaven.

AT THIS TIME

"Take this, this is my Body."
—Mark 14:12–16,22–26

Take me;
I am truly present
for you,
broken for you,
poured out for you,
that you, the many,
might be one.

I will drink it new
when you are present:
broken,
poured out,
for the many,
for the common good
of all.

Chapter 2

REBIRTH

AUTUMN LEAF

There is real beauty
in the Autumn of my life;
not just green,
nor merely yellow,
nor wholly brown,
but variegated.

A touch of green remains,
reminder of my youth;
the child in me
still present.

A trace of yellow lingers
light, fully flickering;
tanned with wisdom,
sunburned brown,
wind-tried and tired,
frosted with rejection.

An Autumn leaf:
torn in some areas
by myself,
or by the weathering
of life itself;
lines of life
more apparent now
than when
I first budded;

yet strong
    straight
    sturdy lines,
stenciled indelibly
in time.

An Autumn leaf
spelling loneliness;
separated from mother tree,
yet lying down
in the midst of
and with
my brother/sister leaves;
huddled together
against whimsical swirls
of Winter wind.

An Autumn leaf,
omen of Winter's death,
devastated,
yet returning
to mother earth
nourishing new life,
believing in Spring.

EASTER LAUGHTER

John 20:1–9

The Christian faith begins, simply enough, with Easter laughter. Yes, laughter! Not the empty, nervous laughter of our society, but the authentic laughter that emanates from the real experience of peace and joy with God's victory over death and creation of new life. The Christian faith begins with the new thing God is doing in and to this dead Jesus of Nazareth to create a new history…and a new world order. Mary Magdalene is the first to laugh the ecstatic laugh of Easter, the first to recognize the ultimate shock of what God has done to death. The laughter of Mary Magdalene at the recognition of our risen Lord is what qualifies this new history as one with a future of joy and victory. From her we must learn this resurrection laughter, because we also live in another history, the history of death and suffering all around us this Easter morning. To regain our nerve and energy as the faithful church of Jesus, we must hear Mary Magdalene's Easter laughter, and be infected by her hope.

She was not the first person to laugh in biblical history. In Genesis, we have the delightful story of Sarah, Abraham's wife, who laughed a cynical laugh when told she would bear a child out of her barrenness. But what a peal of laughter she let out when God *did* create new life in her!

What of our own cynicism? Why are our expectations so limited and our hope so faint? How often do we feel trapped in the barrenness of managing an infertile shell?

Some people among us—especially women in the Church—are beginning to expect the unexpected, are beginning to hear the laughter of Mary Magdalene and are beginning to laugh with her—an indisputable sign that the power of the resurrection *is* creating a faithful people of God, born in newness, born out of the Second Vatican Council.

Why is it Mary, this sinful lady, who first encounters the risen Lord? Why not Peter or John, but this sinful lady who first sees the implications of the resurrection? Why is it she who begins the Easter laughter? It would seem to be that it was because of her tears and the persevering quality of her suffering. Jesus' love transformed Mary's suffering into power; no longer was she bound and vulnerable, no longer definable according to her demons. She changed from being powerlessly passive to being self-contained and receptive. Mary Magdalene was prepared for her laughing by her crying. Evidently she caught on to what God was doing in Jesus somewhat sooner than the theologians and the activists, the religious zealots around Jesus.

Jesus was serious about suffering with the least of his brothers and sisters, and for Mary that meant suffering with Jesus too. Jesus himself became the very least of all when dragged to the execution on the landfill beyond the city.

Who forgot Jesus and turned their backs on him when he and his hopes were reduced to the human rubbish pile? Incredibly, almost everybody. Who stayed? Among the few, we remember Mary of Magdala. She did not forget the one who became the least of all; she stayed and she cried. She stayed until the managers of death had their way, until death itself had its way. And after the death of the one whom she loved more than life, she stayed.

That was more than could be expected of her. Who today stands by those who have been hopelessly claimed by death and death's systems in *our* society? Only those who are free and powerful enough to cry. The others will have retired to a comfortable place to rest and think about it. Who will not let death make its claims? Only those with the freedom to hope against hope and to love in spite of death.

> HER CRYING AND LAUGHTER REMIND US OF GOD'S POWER TO MAKE OUR WEEPING CEASE.

This is the power of Mary Magdalene, who in *God's* ordering of things, is the link between the abomination of Friday afternoon and the incredible joy of Easter morning. Mary Magdalene who weeps in the presence of death, *with hope*, is the one addressed by the living, death-free Lord: "Woman, why are you weeping?" Thus enters the joy that leads us to say, "Even this world of death has a sure future of life." Mary Magdalene was Jesus' friend and companion in the ministry of the Kingdom, the powerful and faithful disciple even unto death, the first witness of the resurrection, and the first proclaimer of the Good News. Her crying and laughter are yet in our ears, reminding us of God's power to make our weeping cease, to turn crying into that laughter which begets in us the fullness of life.

In the fourth century, John Chrysostom said this:

> Let none of us mourn
> that we have fallen
> again and again…
>
> Death has been frustrated,
> for it grabbed a body
> and discovered God.

AT THIS TIME

"We preach Christ crucified…"
—1 Corinthians 1:22–25

While the pious
   demand signs and
wonders
and the humanists
   search for wisdom,
how absurd for us
   to reveal Christ crucified;
how odd to say
   that God's folly
   is wiser than
   conventional wisdom,
or, that God's weakness
   is more powerful
   than our nation's strength.
Do I believe it?

MASS OF THE RESURRECTION
Daniel Richard Allen

Amos 5:7–13, 21–24; James 5:1–6; Matthew 25:31–40

If I believed in reincarnation, I would have to suspect that James (the author of the Epistle) has come back as Dan Allen, and perhaps Amos came back as James, and, appropriately, James is the least popular of the major New Testament writers. Small wonder. For James, like Dan (and, of course, like Jesus), bases his teaching of justice upon the fundamental distinction between the rich and the poor. God's love comes close to the poor and lowly, the least of the brothers and sisters. The rich must find a way of standing at their side if they, too, are to know God's acceptance. In Christ, according to James and Dan, *all* are equal; nevertheless, if God could be said to have favorites, it would be the poor who would be singled out for God's predilection. To draw close to the poor by coming to their aid is equivalent, in James' and Dan's view, to drawing close to God. In Dan's own words (25 years ago) from the original mission statement of Neighbor for Neighbor, he put it this way: "We are changing the attitude of the affluent. Their contact with the poor makes them aware that they, the affluent, have created the poor, therefore, they can recreate, both in the society of the poor and in their own environment."

As one of Dan's nephews put it, "Dan was *above all* a teacher." He was *above all* a teacher because he was *below it all*: streetwise, incarnate among the poor; he was there, *present!* (He understood; that is, stood under, not over.)

Dan did not practice what he preached—he preached what he practiced. He was what he practiced; it came from his very being, and that's why he appeared so authentic, so real, because he *was*. (It was a graced gift he was open to.)

James and Dan call us to look carefully at our own *interior* attitudes and to ask just how they are reflected in *what we do*. They insist that our faith has to be enfleshed, if it is to have credibility. Dan looks at corporate America and says with James: "Behold the worker's wage …kept back from them by you …calls out against you!" Matthew's parable speaks of the least of Christ's brothers and sisters. Down at the farm where Dan, Pickett and I spent twenty years of Mondays, Dan's concern for the least was vividly seen. When he mowed the acreage he was extremely careful not to mow down any weed that was blooming. The rich variety of blooming weeds fascinated him far more than the normal ordinary flowers that we care for. This innate sensibility was obviously reflected in Dan's association with the *least* of the poor—those who simply ceased to exist, for example, as economic persons, invisible to all lending institutions.

> DAN DID NOT PRACTICE WHAT HE PREACHED— HE PREACHED WHAT HE PRACTICED.

The last thing Dan said to me, the night before surgery as I was leaving—he turned in the doorway and said, "Bill, pray for me." Dan was a believer with substance. As reported by Father Monahan in the magazine *Salt of the Earth*, Dan understood Eucharist to be for the sake of those present, so they will become God's love for the many. When we say in the Eucharist, "This is my body, my blood for you and for the many," all too often we forget about the many. For Dan they were the many of "I was hungry, I was naked."

It could be said that Dan used colorful language. Well, yes, but he swore about something decent. He swore out of justified anger, because the "least" were getting less. *We* swear because we, who already have too much, want more.

Monahan again says it well: "Dan Allen's bearded face is a mosaic of the sadness of poverty provoked by damaging greed, and an articulate sense of humor, which bubbles up from a deep well of hope in the reign of God."

There was a splendid editorial in the *Tulsa World* this morning on Dan. Let me share with you the last two paragraphs:

> "To those who didn't know him, the gruff and plain-spoken Allen may have seemed an unlikely candidate to be the chief advocate for local poor people. But to those who knew him well, those traits and others made him the lovable and unforgettable character that he was.
>
> "The people who Allen brought on board and trained in poverty-fighting techniques no doubt

will try hard to carry out the vision that the once-dubbed 'radical priest' strived for his entire adult life. They will succeed, because his dedication, enthusiasm and timelessness were infectious. But they will never replace him. Dan Allen was one of a kind."

Jesus said that whoever cared for the "least" would enter eternal life. This morning Jesus is saying, "Welcome, Dan, into the Kingdom, for wherever I am there you will be."

DYING ALIVE

2 Corinthians 4:7–12

"Some people claim there is no life after death," said a disciple.

"Do they?" said the Master noncommittally.

Said the disciple: "Wouldn't it be awful to die—and never again see or hear or love or move?"

"You find that awful?" said the Master. "But that's how most people are even before they die."

—Anthony de Mello

I would like to share some thoughts about dying, *while* we are living, in order that when we do die, we will die alive and not die dead.

Lent is a journey into and through the mystery of Jesus' death and resurrection. This is a faith event.

It is not to be proved. Jesus died and was raised from death by the Father. The only proof is the testimony of Christianity. Since this dual event is a seeming contradiction, a paradox, understanding can best be grasped through analogy: like out of winter comes spring—not from it, not following it, but *out* of it. No spring without winter.

"Whoever would save their lives will lose them, but whoever loses their lives will find them." Paradox! Mystery! Out of loss comes gain, discovery. That line would not play in Peoria or Wall Street.

> JESUS WAS ALREADY DEAD WHEN HE DIED—DEAD, THAT IS, TO HIMSELF.

Our Lenten journey has three stopovers: Holy Thursday, Good Friday, Easter Sunday. The first a supper celebration of a reality that has been going on for years: his being spent, broken and poured out for his friends. Paradox: no unity can come from bread unless it is *first broken*, *then* shared.

Good Friday: the ultimate brokenness—his death for us. And out of his death, life. An incredible paradox: Easter Sunday. Without Good Friday, *no* Easter Sunday. Without a life being spent for others, without a life being broken for others, without a life being poured out for others, there would have been no *saving* Good Friday. His death was a summing up, an accumulative finalization of many dyings in his life…that others might live. Jesus was already dead when he died—dead, that is, to himself. He was what

Chapter 2 • Rebirth

he proclaimed. He spent his entire public *life* losing it for the sake of others. The "bottom line" was resurrection. A correlative paradox is this: In a sense, Jesus' real birthday was not Christmas but Easter Sunday. On Christmas God experiences a human coming to be…a dying to divinity, a total immersion into our humanity. But on Easter, Jesus in his very humanity became Lord of the universe. Jesus' humanity, *through* and *out of* his death, was born into the fullness of life with his Father. What does this mean for us? As God became immersed in humanity, we, through baptism, were immersed in divinity, plunged into Jesus' risen humanity, and into the mystery of his death and resurrection. His Kingdom is both anticipated and in process. He is coming to be life-giving *now*, not by and by in the sky, through us, his Body, the church.

Our baptism is our Christmas feast. Inspirited by the Lord we begin our personal journey to the Father, in Christ, within the Christian community, who journey with us. As persons of faith when we die, we should already be dead…dead, that is, to ourselves. Our *death* should be our Easter feast. That's why we can "celebrate" death.

In 2 Corinthians 4:7–12, Paul says, "Continually we carry about in our bodies the dying of Jesus, so that in our bodies the life of Jesus may also be revealed. Death is at work in us, but life in you." Death should be at work in us, but life in our families and all those whose lives we touch. To be life-giving, one must die. To live then, paradoxically involves a life-long process of dying, *and* coming to life. Death and resurrection are happening to us every moment of our lives, if our relationships are lovingly and responsibly managed…if we truly *see* or *hear* or *love* or *move* for the sake of others.

We are resurrected, like Lazarus,

whenever someone unties us and lets us go free,

when someone trusts us—lets us be ourselves in their presence,

when someone is there for us in difficult times with or without words,

when someone understands and affirms us no matter what trial or limitation we may be experiencing.

We, in turn, bring the reality of resurrection into the lives of others as we are willing to be spent, broken, and poured out for them. In all our relationships we should be able to say, "Death is at work in me, but life in you." There is nothing morbid here. Fullness cannot happen without emptiness. To be full of ourselves is deadly, a deadliness that cannot give life. The rugged individualism, central to our culture, begets racism, greed, violence—signs of the presence of evil.

The paradox of death and resurrection takes flesh in what we think are the most insignificant exchanges: simply listening to someone in trouble, standing with the afflicted or oppressed when we cast our ballots, or maybe even winking at a homely girl.

Chapter 2 • Rebirth

CHRIST-LIKE IN THE WORLD

Genesis 15:5–12,17,18; Philippians 3:17–4:1; Luke 9:28–36

The mountain: what would it be like being a mountain? Just imagine it! I am lofty, immovable, immense, silent, difficult to ascend, to reach, aloof, barren at my summit, serene. That fits, doesn't it?

There really is a dimension of myself (and yourselves) that transcends, or wants to get above the noise, the babel, the petty things that make up much of life…the cooking, the buying, the taxiing, the chattering. There is a mountain me that wants to rise above it all, and live serenely, unperturbed, beyond involvement; perched above, able to see all, to detect all, thus able to judge all and avoid all, never needing to change, to react, to respond. Content only to observe the world around *me*, take distant and objective note of all things and people, or ignore them as my fancy dictates. There is the apathetic, perfectionist me who finds life too aimless at ground level; the insecure me that needs to see it all, know it all, control it all from above and beyond the painful reach of life, from above and beyond the flat land that seems to level everyone…where one's visibility, prominence, identity is lost amid so many pushy people, so many details, so many demands.

No, I prefer to be a mountain, prominent (at least in my own mind) and superior, unmoved…the focal point of all, secure, still.

Now *that* sounds like health and wholeness. That sounds so Christ-like: to be that transcendent; to ascend the mountain, to seek that vantage point and from there, transfigured, to bestow myself with saintly selectivity upon the world…to do good without mistakes, to think and speak infallibly, to be pure and correct in *all* I do, always right, never wrong. Amen! Alleluia!

Simon Peter buys the package. "Hold it," he says, looking at Moses, Elijah and Jesus, with video camera in hand. "Don't lose that pose! This mountain is a good place to be, folks. After all, what are health and wholeness all about, if not the absence of pain and mortality and error and worry? Forget Jerusalem! Forget the journey! Let's build three bed-and-breakfasts here on the mountaintop and settle down."

How easily we forget one of Luke's singular features in the story: that as Jesus enters the cloud with Elijah and Moses it disappears *without* him *in* it, and represents a refusal on his part to accept glory without suffering. Jesus understood his call—his election—not as assuring glory, but as an invitation to place his life at the disposal of the poor, the imprisoned, the blind and lame of history, of *all* of *us*. The passion was not merely accepted or endured by Jesus, it was a *deliberate* passion, a *chosen* passion.

Poor Peter, like most of us, is too full of his own assumptions about health and wholeness to hear what Jesus is saying: that the mountain is Christ's point of *departure*, not arrival; the mountain is a place *from which* he *descends* to experience all the things that we *ascend* to escape: like misunderstanding, anxiety, rejection, lay-offs, conflicting opinions, the abuse of authority by cautious or lazy people, brutality, tears, pain, death. If I want to be whole, then I can't settle down on this peaceful mountain. That's precisely what the church did, prior to Vatican II: sat on a mountaintop for 500 years…and sat there triumphantly! (Looking down its Roman nose at all those Protestants.)

If I want my Christ-self to emerge, I have to come *down* the mountain *with him* for if I would save my life, I would lose it, but in losing my life, *to let Christ emerge*, I will save it. Lent is a time of immersion: Baptism…a time to come off the mountain and immerse myself, just as I am, *in the world*, to pick up the discarded pieces; to embrace, despite all my reluctance, the me that is just so high, and whose arms stretch out just so wide; to embrace the me that is ignorant, that knows so little and assumes so much; to embrace the me that is worried, impatient, that wants everyone else to be prompt, alert, caring, non-judgmental; the me that falls far short of all these standards myself; to embrace the me that is inconsistent, that wants to love and be loved, but remains cautious; the me that pleases people, but never quite pleases my conscience; the me that hurts people but can't admit it.

THE MOUNTAIN IS CHRIST'S POINT OF *DEPARTURE*, NOT ARRIVAL.

Wholeness and health of spirit requires *that immersion*, that coming down, that incarnation. To let Christ emerge is not to be *other* than I am, but to embrace *what I am* with *mercy*. Mercy, not pity, is the basic ingredient for the emerging Christ-self.

Mercy doesn't directly change things; it relaxes things, and out of relaxation who knows what wonderful things could happen. But we still seem to believe that it is *our* efforts which count more than anything else. This is a reversal, of course, of what the gospel proclaims: the whole biblical story of Abraham's election, the birth of Jesus from a virgin, the raising of Christ crucified, reflects clearly the good news of the absolute freedom and gratuity of the gift of God's love in creation and redemption.

> BECOMING CHRIST-CENTERED REQUIRES A KIND OF DYING.

Somehow, we have all remained convinced that we can *merit* the gift, that God *needs* us to need the gift, that unless we work to *deserve* it, we can never be sure that God really means to give it. And so, we boot-strap Catholics don't find it easy to relax, to be merciful to ourselves and others. We have been taught too many distinctions, we have become too principled, too law-centered for that. So becoming merciful, and therefore becoming Christ-centered, requires a kind of dying—a sacrifice of the tidiness we impose on ourselves and reality. Lent offers the community in troubled, dark times, the light of opportunity to experience that dying, which, strangely enough, can make us quite well.

AT THIS TIME

"The one who believes has eternal life…"
—John 6:41–51

Eternal life
does not happen
by and by
in the sky
when we die;
it happens now
when I believe
and when I become
(in Christ)
bread broken
for others.

JESUS LIVES, ALLELUIA

1 Corinthians 5:6–8; John 20:1–9

*I*f we judge life by literature, we would have to conclude that life has more pains than pleasures. Daily conversation reinforces that conclusion. People talk endlessly about their woes and shortchange their joys. It is evidently easier to talk about sad things than about happy things. Sadness lingers but joy is fleeting. That is the problem at the heart of our Easter celebration. After a lifetime of apparent failure, Jesus rose to a new life in an instant. We have spent Lent and Holy Week recalling Jesus' passion and death. Now, what else is there to say except "Alleluia!" That is not even a word for us—it is just a joyful sound: Alleluia! We have no words to express our joy adequately. Is that because we do not expect much joy in life and therefore we have not bothered to invent the words to express it? Or is it because joy is an emotion that goes beyond words, transcends description?

So what makes us joyful today? (Or are we?) What are we celebrating? The joy that tugs at our spirits as we remember and reflect on a victorious event in ancient history: resurrection. Does that make you joyful remembering the resurrection? Doesn't do much for me. Jesus did win a victory but we can never fully lose ourselves in the joy of another person, nor get excited about an event of history. Easter proclaims the *present* tense: that *his* victory is also *ours*…Jesus' resurrection is always now!…that we too *will* rise from the dead. Here the joy may become more personal and immediate. But we are too tied to the temporal to get overly excited about eternity. Too impatient with things that must be done now to rejoice over something that we think is in the sky by and by.

Jesus never promised to overcome all sickness or war or stupidity—look as his apostles! He only claimed the power to overcome death. The world is not noticeably different since his resurrection because God cannot change the facts of life without destroying the humanness of life. The difference Easter makes is that death is no longer the end of life. We do not have two lives—one now, then one later—anymore than a cat has nine lives. We have only one life. Resurrection means that death is not a period, but a comma—a pause to make sense out of life. Death is like a rest in a musical score: it recapitulates the notes already played and anticipates the ones to come, hopefully notes of greater joy! To be mundane about it—death is a coffee break.

We too easily presume that *death* is the major factor of life—the great leveler that finally invalidates all we do. From that point of view, resurrection is merely a consolation prize—a palatable aftermath to the real business of living in this world—a cushion. Small wonder so many people opt for reincarnation as a solution. Well, God bless Shirley MacLaine, but on Easter we proclaim a different reality. Jesus' resurrection proves that *life* is the major fact of existence. *In Jesus* our *lives* are uninterrupted continuums. Death and resurrection are equally real—human experiences in our endless life process as we see in the banner and cross. That *belief* should give a different dimension to life—a thrilling new thrust that puts death in its *subordinate* place—and let us live more fully. At least it's a heady idea. It flashes all about us this day—

> in the flame of candles
> in the sparkle of water
> in the beauty of flowers

in the color of wine
in a new moon and longer days
and the texture of bread.

    This is not a day for *speaking* of joy, but *singing* it. This is the season to dare new visions because all the old are dead. But Jesus lives—Alleluia! and so do we—Alleluia!

Chapter 3

FAITH in CHRIST

A Funny Thing Happened on the Way to Being Church

We need to smile
   to ourselves;
laugh a little
    at how well
    we miss
    the gospel point,
    for the point
    is often painful.

We all want to
"follow" Jesus
through his teaching,
   his doctrine,
   his words,
but rarely through
   his life-style,
   his behavior,
   his poverty,
   his values.

Jesus didn't practice
   what he preached;
   he preached
   what he practiced.

The Word came out of
   his experiences,

> his relationships
> (who he was,
> not what he was).

Jesus didn't think about
> what he was doing;
> he did
> what he thought about.

We need to do
> what Jesus did,
> not just think
> what he thought
> (to become a who,
> not a what).

If we do
what he did
we will come to think
as he thought:

He ignored
> this world's wisdom,
he sought no power,
> bought no home,
praised compassion
> over worship,
> need over wealth.
He reflected on
> the lilies of the field,
> not political favor.

We are on
> an orthodoxy kick
> (right doctrine)

  instead of orthopraxy
  (right doing).

We too easily
  affirm his divinity,
  but deny, in practice,
  his incarnation.

We have firm beliefs,
  but little application,
  forgetting that faith
  is a verb,
  not a noun.

Yes, funny things happen…

Chapter 3 • Faith in Christ

VOLUNTARY DARKNESS
John 17:1–11

*I*f Jesus became incarnate in the world of our time, within our present cultural and social system, it might well be played out this way. I have before me something resembling a personnel report. It states:

> Memorandum To: Jesus, son of Joseph
> From: Jordan Management
>   Consultants, Inc.
>
> Dear Sir:
> Thank you for submitting the names of the twelve men you have picked for managerial positions. All of them have completed our tests and have undergone extensive personal interviews with both our psychologist and vocational aptitude consultant. Copies of their completed profiles are enclosed. It is our opinion, Sir, that most of your nominees are lacking in the necessary educational background and aptitude for your enterprise. They do not understand the "team" concept.
>
> Simon Peter is emotionally unstable, impulsive, and given to fits of temper. Andrew possesses no leadership qualities whatsoever. The two brothers, James and John, place personal interest above company loyalty. Thomas demonstrates a questioning attitude that would tend to undermine morale. We feel it is our duty to advise you that Matthew has been blacklisted by the Greater Jerusalem Better Business Bureau. James, son of Alphaeus, and Simon (who admits membership in

the Zealot Party) have radical leanings and could be considered left-wing agitators.

Only one of the candidates shows great potential. He is a man of ability and resourcefulness, who meets people well and has a keen business sense. He is a member of the Jerusalem Chamber of Commerce. He is highly motivated, ambitious and responsible. We recommend as your comptroller and executive vice-president, Judas Iscariot.

All other profiles are self-explanatory. Wishing you every success in your new venture.

Sincerely yours,

Jordan Management Consultants, Inc.

The apostles were, obviously, quite ordinary people, with ordinary warts and blemishes…like ourselves. They were people who, until the resurrection-Pentecost events seemed to have a love for the dark, who didn't appear to *want* to know. We all know folks like this: There is the child who puts her fingers in her ears when something unpleasant is told to her. There are those who cannot hear anything wrong about their children. There are those who simply refuse to see the world as the world is, who escape from the outer drama of our human lives, to the inner drama of their fantasies. They have ears, Jesus said, but they do not hear. They have eyes but they do not see. They have hands but they do not feel.

This is *voluntary darkness* and unwillingness to see—and unwillingness to learn. *Voluntary darkness* occurs when people *like me*, who are over-rich and overweight, discuss hunger and poverty in the world. *Voluntary darkness* happens when students discuss justice and equality, while hating their teachers or ignoring fellow students. I remember one time about twenty years ago when Father Bob Pickett and I were on vacation visiting his sister, an Army nurse, in Mesa, Arizona. We were lounging around the swimming pool drinking expensive scotch and discussing the problem of hunger and poverty in the world. That is *voluntary darkness*. *Voluntary darkness* when we freely discuss the Kingdom of God, while forgetting that God is to be found among the poor in Spirit.

Voluntary darkness happened in epidemic amounts around Jesus. Peter did not see and told Jesus that he should not suffer. James and John did not see, so they asked him, "Can't we be in charge?" Thomas did not see, and said, "I don't believe!" Philip did not see, and asked, "Show us the Father!" The Sadducees did not see. The Pharisees did not see. His own family did not see; they thought he was crazy. It was as if *nobody* saw.

Jesus prays to the Father, but what he says is also meant for his disciples: "Father, now *at last* they *know* the teaching you gave me, and they have accepted it." The darkness has seen the light. (The farewell address is written from a post-resurrection understanding.) What about ourselves? What about me? about you? Are we prepared to know Christ's truth—not merely the world's? Are we prepared to understand our *real* situation as Catholics in a troubled world? To be responsible for the "common good" of all and not merely the good of a few?

When he left, they went back to the upper room. They prayed, waiting for insight, for truth, hoping to be healed, to become whole. On Pentecost the Spirit of Jesus enlightened them.

The hour has come for us, too,
time to give life to the world around us in *all* our relationships.

It's time to face the pain and anguish;
to experience the joy and gladness;
to touch life with gentleness;
to learn wisdom—Christ's wisdom, not the world's;
to be open, to risk, to live on the edge:
to be truly *in* the world but not *of* it…
so that hopefully, the world of unbelief,
the world veiled in darkness, will come to believe, to see, to hear;
will come to change,
will come to transformation,
will come to be itself—a sign of God's splendor and glory.

KEEP HOPE ALIVE

Wisdom 12:13,16–19; Romans 8:26,27; Matthew 13:24–30

> *A woman dreamed she walked into a brand-new section of a produce market and, to her surprise, found God behind the counter. "What do you sell here?" she inquired. "Everything your heart desires," said God. Hardly daring to believe what she was hearing, the woman decided to ask for the best things a human could wish*

> *for. "I want peace of mind and love and happiness and wisdom and freedom from fear," she said. Then as an afterthought, she added, "Not just for me, for everyone on earth." God smiled. "I think you've got me wrong, my dear. We don't sell fruits here, only seeds."*
>
> —Anthony de Mello

And so we experience the weeds and the wheat growing together from seedlings. The field of the gospel corresponds well to the world as we know it: a confusing mix of good and evil, a world where bad things happen to good people…and good things happen to bad people. Jesus, speaking in parable, is obviously more concerned with helping us *cope* rather than explaining *why* it is the way it is. The gospel assures us that the evil that comes our way is not God's doing but "an enemy hand." This helps us to retain our identity as people loved by God. Whatever evil befalls us, it is *not* God's punishment or desire.

The gospel story acknowledges that evil is painfully close, and this reality is not likely to change. It's obvious also that we ourselves are not pure wheat, but part weed. We may not be the worst in comparison to some others, but nevertheless we do *not* have our Kingdom act together. As we get older, and hopefully wiser, experience teaches us to pin more of our hopes on God's presence and power than on our own determined efforts.

The reading from the book of Wisdom suggests two thoughts: God cares compassionately for all—

even the evil doer. God also expects us to love all—*even the evil doer.* As we try to accomplish this profound and rather preposterous task, we quickly come to the end of our human powers. We are confronted by our own evil and arrive upon a frontier where the only power left to rely on is God's. This frontier seems to be the place where God has chosen to ready us for the harvest. Although this is not particularly comfortable or pleasant, it has one tremendous advantage: this frontier tells us that the reign of God does take root in the crannies of our limits, our weaknesses.

> GOD CARES COMPASSIONATELY FOR ALL —EVEN THE EVIL DOER.

This is not a question of just "hanging in there." The Kingdom is at hand within us. We are summoned to keep hope alive. And that requires a kind of "bifocal" vision. We must, in faith, clearly see both the sometimes unpleasant shapes of our present experience and, at the same time, see the Kingdom coming with its victory. A bifocal vision helps us to discern: we learn when to watch and pray, and when to put our hands to the plow. We come to find large courage in little successes. We discover by surprise that we *are* steadfast—clear in vision and rooted in compassion.

This is not a popular approach in a culture of pragmatism. Results now, not vision, is the rule of our age. Yet, there are exceptions—two persons who witness to life *lived by vision*: Vaclav Havel of Czechoslovakia and Nelson Mandela of South Africa. During the years of setbacks, imprisonment, isolation and very few results, these two must have wondered whether God was cruel and uncaring about their predicament. Much more than any of us, keeping hope alive for them was a daily struggle with pain that caused, as Paul puts it, "groaning which cannot be expressed in speech." Mandela asserted, "Yes, it is worth it to go to prison because of your convictions, and being prepared to suffer for what you believe in is something worthwhile. It is an achievement for a person to do his or her duty on earth irrespective of the consequences." Both Mandela and Havel have bifocal vision.

Confronted with evil and pain we are tempted to doubt and fatalism, which leads to what Havel called "reprehensible passivity." Another temptation is self-righteousness: "the world is divided into heroes and villains and thank God, *we're* heroes."

The lives of Havel and Mandela suggest another direction: Keep hope alive with a bifocal vision. Remain realists in seeing the present situation. Strategies are determined not by short-term goals but by heeding what one hears: a gospel promise that the victory is not in doubt...for those who hold to the vision. We must continue to replace hate with love, injustice with faith, isolation with community, violence with healing. We must continue to keep compassionate company with those who painfully experience the reign of evil; hopefully, we will not keep company with those who dish it out.

Nothing surpasses the holiness of those who have learned perfect acceptance of everything that is. The poet Auden wrote something like this: "If I shout at the sky about the state of the world, the sky would only wait until my breath was gone and then it would repeat—as if I had said nothing—repeat its standing order, Bless whatever is."

The humble role of the Christian is not to presume to construct God's Kingdom but to make ourselves fit to live there. Can we trust the seed to grow? Can we let God be God and stick to our own task—keeping hope alive? Are we content simply to bless *whatever* God lets be? For that will be the Kingdom of God.

AT THIS TIME

"Are we aware that we who were baptized into Christ Jesus were baptized into His death?"
—ROMANS 6:3,4,8–11

I doubt it,
since I don't seem to believe
in dying to myself,
much less in living for others.

Many of us, apparently,
will die dead
when we die,
instead of dying alive
"in Christ Jesus."

Chapter 3 • Faith in Christ

GLORY & PEACE ON EARTH
Isaiah 9:1–3,5,6; Titus 2:11–14; Luke 2:1–4

Christmas is the beginning of a new time. This day the longing of Advent is fulfilled and a future is given to us. This day will tell again the story of God's blessing: a boy-king is born in Bethlehem. This story is for all humankind the most *wonder*-ful. It is Emmanuel—the truth of the promise God made in ages past, to dwell among us. And the angels told the shepherds: "Do not be afraid!" The power and the "*otherness*" of the creator God has come among us as a *child* to redeem our goodness and to end our exile.

Christmas is a light shining from afar. No human darkness is stronger than that light; no human loneliness greater than that love that sent a child to share our poverty and insecurity, to share our fear of Caesar and the rulers of this world.

This is why Jesus is called *Savior*. He is the *presence* of God—

> God's wisdom incarnate
>
> God's love enfleshed
>
> God's mercy embodied.

In him, God's justice and peace embrace; Jesus, the God-hero, now also human, who alone brings joy to all people. Wrapped in swaddling clothes at birth, in a swaddling shroud at death, he will live and die…to make us whole, fulfilled, to free us from every bondage that self and human lack and political or corporate climate can inflict.

This is what we have gathered to remember these troubled days: the mystery of God who comes as Father and Mother to the world in the life and deeds, in the way and truth of Jesus.

And the angels said: "Do not be afraid!" But we *are* afraid—not of the angels singing, but of our own fixed notions, our myopic vision, that a child is not strong enough to contradict the world. We are afraid of our vulnerabilities: the desire we have to live comfortable rather than good lives. We are afraid to admit that the needs of the poor should take priority over the wants of the rich, that the freedom of the dominated takes priority over the liberty of the powerful, that the participation of the marginalized takes priority over the preservation of an order that excludes them. The child Jesus entered this world poor, dominated, marginalized, but the risen Jesus has the power to contradict that world.

That is why we sentimentalize Christmas. This is why we want to maintain the baby Jesus in a crib. It is because sweetness, a sugary facade, is a mask for human weakness.

The parish Women's Club asked me a year ago if I could find a new crib for the church at Christmas. I thought about that and about St. James, and I thought of all the sugary sweet Jesuses I've seen in my life, and all the bad and schlock kitsch art I've seen in churches, and so I thought some more and went to a chain saw artist. Isn't that fascinating? Who else but a nut like me would go to a chain saw artist? Marvelous man, Clayton Coss—a little too reverent for me, but we got along fine. The first sketch he gave me

Chapter 3 • Faith in Christ

had a dear old St. Joseph with folded hands looking down on sweet Jesus, and I said, "I don't like it." He said, "Father, it has to be reverent," and I said, "No, it should be irreverent." Between his reverence and my irreverence, Mary turned out reverent and we ended up with a laughing cow. So, whatever, it seems to fit St. James.

We are desperately afraid that we have no resources to help one another, and we know that *our* strength and wisdom is not enough. But today our weariness is surprised and our senses enlivened.

This child was warmed to life in a stable (not a palace). Human love and animal breath was all God's child needed to give healing and light to a troubled world. Do we need so much more than that?

Today we ask God's blessing on bread and wine that *human* hands have made, and we believe that the intimate presence of our God transforms our words and actions. Divine life comes once more to birth in human hearts; the Eucharist empowers us to become the body and blood of Christ in the world. The eternal Word and Bread of Life is our strength and our gift—our reason not to fear the darkness, or the need we see reflected in each other's eyes.

> THE INTIMATE PRESENCE OF OUR GOD TRANSFORMS OUR WORDS AND ACTIONS.

Rejoice in this perfect love that gives itself for our communion and oneness. *This* is glory and peace on earth! Merry Christmas!

MYSELF IN CHRIST

Baruch 5:1–9; Philippians 1:4–6,8–11; Luke 3:1–6

PROPHECY:
"I wish to become a teacher of the Truth." "Are you prepared to be ridiculed, ignored and starved till you are sixty-five?" "I am. But tell me: What will happen after I am sixty-five?" "You will have grown accustomed to it."

—ANTHONY DE MELLO

In playwright Henrik Ibsen's An Enemy of the People, *a small town has discovered that a nearby brook is really a mineral spring. The townspeople build a health spa over the spring and look forward to fame and fortune as a health resort. But the doctor in the village discovers that the water also contains a bacteria that will cause many people to become sick and perhaps die. The doctor reports his findings to the people. But instead of thanking and supporting the doctor, the people turn against him for publicizing his findings and destroying their plans to profit from the springs. Instead of emerging a hero, the doctor becomes "an enemy of the people."*

—CONNECTIONS

Prophets like the doctor and John the Baptizer challenge us to see our lives beyond the narrow confines of self. They call us to look beyond legalisms and the bottom line to see what is right, what is authentically good, what is God.

The ancient proclamation of John the Baptist is that we are living without God, ignoring God and God's demands. This life that takes God lightly is destroying us (if we look around), for it shoves God to the margins of life and makes God irrelevant in terms of how we do business in family, work and politics. John is angry at the sense of waste—a sad senselessness, the stubborn unseeing willfulness (for example, the war in Yugoslavia).

He proclaims a "baptism of repentance": a call to change, a turning away from the wiles of the world, to doing God's will. Destruction will come—if it does come—not from a vengeful, inhuman and vindictive God, but from the natural consequences of living, cut off from life's very source...of trying to be human without that which makes us human. We don't seem to grasp that it is precisely our intimacy with God that continually *re*-creates us to become *who* we are, the *who God* wants us to be. It would seem that God is present to us only in the option, the choice, by which we open ourselves to the infinite. Every one of us, male or female, is carried forward—as was the Baptizer—to the inevitable choice between a saving faith and self-destructive idolatry. Either I open myself to the infinite and thereby become more truly myself, or I refuse to follow the divine invitation, attach myself to a finite reality (whatever—success, money, power) and block my quest for true fulfillment.

John, open to the infinite, was enabled to be his own person, and therefore able and free to be a prophet. Anyone who dieted on grasshoppers and wild honey couldn't be *too* attached to many conventional values. Paradoxically, John was able to be prophetic because his identity wasn't wrapped up in being a prophet. His identity—being himself, John—was in his own personhood, a personhood open to the infinite…to God's intimate presence in his life, an experience that came to him in the wilderness—the desert, where there are no distractions. John was led "by the light of God's glory, with God's mercy and justice for company."

A personal reflection: In observing a number of priests experiencing a great deal of stress in their lives, I have often suspected that their lives are stressful primarily because they try too hard to be priests, and get locked into some kind of institutional vision of what priests should or ought to be. A solution seems to be that if they would simply be themselves-in-Christ, they would turn out to be better priests-in-Christ and find it less stressful.

To be myself-in-Christ, whether priest or truck driver, means to pursue my own truth in relation to Christ's values, values found in Matthew 5, the Sermon on the Mount: poverty of Spirit; lowliness; single heartedness; being a peacemaker; sorrowing for a troubled world; thirsting for justice; turning the cheek; sharing the shirt or blouse; walking the extra mile; giving to those who beg from me; letting myself be led "by the light of God's glory, with God's mercy and justice for company." This will, of course, bring conflict and ridicule, but with some time set aside for the desert, time for prayer and reflection, time to be open to the infinite, I will grow accustomed to it, and hopefully be me—the me God wants me to be.

QUIET—BE STILL

Job 38:8–11; Mark 4:35–41

It's a beautiful day in the park and the young father is pushing his screaming child in his stroller. As the father wheels his infant son along their path, he keeps murmuring, "Easy now, Donald. Just keep calm, Donald. It's all right, Donald. Just relax, Donald. It's gonna be all right, Donald…"

A woman passes by and says to the young father, "You certainly know how to talk to an upset child—quietly and gently." The woman leans over the stroller and coos, "What seems to be the trouble, Donald?"

And the father says, "Oh no, no. He's Henry, I'm Donald."

—Connections

Throughout our own journeys through life we encounter "storms"—some of the storms we experience are minor squalls, like Henry's, others are catastrophic typhoons. Within each of us is that voice of Jesus: "Be still."

In spite of the watery connection, the selection from Job seems almost trivial compared to the Gospel. But, let me take you in a little deeper to experience the writer's poetic description of God's power. Here are some verses that immediately follow today's first reading:

> "Have *you* ever in *your* life given orders to the morning or sent the dawn to its post, telling it to grasp the earth by its edges and shake the wicked out of it, when it changes the earth to sealing clay and dyes it as we dye clothes; sealing the light from the wicked and braking the arm raised to strike? Have *you* journeyed all the way to the sources of the sea, or walked where the Abyss is deepest? Have *you* been shown the gates of death or met the janitors of Shadowland? Have *you* an inkling of the extent of the earth? Tell me all about it if you have! Which is the way to the home of the light, and where does darkness live? *You* could then show them the way to their proper places, or put them on the path to where they live! If *you* know all this, you must have been born with them, you must be very old by now!"

God seems to be telling his questioner, "Look Job, see how big I am and how small you are! Aren't you out of your league asking *me* questions or daring to ask me the reason about anything?" To the listener this might seem unfair. We are all perplexed by unjust or undeserved suffering. But the author of Job does not mean to make God sound arrogant. The author is really saying to us, "*Look* at the mystery of creation: a bird in flight, a waterfall, a seedling that becomes a giant tree—all these have a density and complexity of being. And we have not even mentioned the human, the greatest marvel of all. All this is the Creator's doing, and the Creator's gift to us." If pain and suffering are part of it, and transiency, too—for this shall pass away, and all of us who behold it—is this reason to reject the Giver of existence itself, the One who framed our lives—however short or long? It is not right to suspect, even to anticipate, that the creative power behind all this is not ended but just beginning, and has power to make right whatever is now perceived by us as wrong? The author of Job was a poet whose work has helped us to think this way. Today it could be a scientist who confronts us with the mystery of being, which is far more extensive and "multi-layered" than our ancestors could have imagined.

In a pre-scientific age, someone close to nature, like an American Indian, could give due reverence to creation and that presence or being which includes us and sustains us. But somewhere we lost the way or the ability to join creation and Creator—things seen and unseen—knowledge and wisdom.

The Gospel describes a group of people out at sea terrified by a storm, fearful of dying. That's a parallel, obviously, to the human situation. We often feel we are "all at sea," bewildered by life or the unfair and tragic things that happen.

The storms that buffet us may be anguish or doubt or grief, money or domestic troubles—whatever. And certainly there is fear of dying. So what are we going to say?

The God worshipped by Job is not a God who gives goodies or satisfactory answers to questions about this life. *This God gives Godself.* The essence of faith, then, is this: the God whom we worship today gives much more than answers to human questions; our God gives a divine relationship, and how marvelous that relationship is. Within each of us is that voice of Jesus: "Be still."

> MAY WE ALWAYS… BE ABLE TO DISCERN THE PRESENCE OF GOD AMID THE WINDS OF DESPAIR AND CONFUSION.

May we always have the wisdom, patience and grace to listen to that voice: to be able to discern the presence of God amid the winds of despair and confusion, to be able to hear the voice of God amid the roar of anger and mistrust, to be able to see the light of God in the darkness of selfishness and prejudice.

Christ is awake within us, saying: "Quiet! Be still!"

Chapter 4

COMMUNITY

TRINITY

Because "God is love,"
God is three,
a plurality,
a community,
a trinity of persons
existing in relationships
of knowing and loving:
the lover/Creator,
the beloved/Redeemer,
love itself/Sanctifier;
three, yet one,
the One for the Many.

We, who believe in God,
who is Trinity,
are created,
redeemed,
sanctified
in that image and likeness;
summoned in baptism
to transcend
our individualities,
go beyond them
into communities
of knowing and loving
where the many
are becoming one
because we are one

Chapter 4 • Community

for the many:
for to deny community
is to deny
our very selves
("...love your neighbor
 as you love yourself").

We who believe
in America,
unfortunately sing
"My country 'tis of Me,"
while celebrating
our individualism,
America's basic
habit of the heart,
whose nature
is to be
anti-trinity:
without relationships
(unless exclusively)
of knowing and loving,
notions silenced
in the noise
of rampant greed
and racism,
where the one rich
are not for
the many poor,

The Trinity
will not be reality
for anyone
until we (myself)

change our tune
to sing:
"My country 'tis
of Thee and We"
(inclusively),
renewing
an old habit
of the heart:
unconditional
positive regard
for everyone,
hopefully recreating
a society
that looks
a little more
like Christ
in community,
knowing and loving:
signs of
our triune God
whose kingdom comes
creating,
redeeming,
sanctifying
the world.

Chapter 4 • Community

FAITH IS A VERB

*Exodus 22:20–26; 1 Thessalonians 1:5–10;
Matthew 22:34–40*

The Master met a newly married couple who asked him: "What shall we do to make our love endure?" The Master replied: "Love other things together."

—Anthony de Mello

There are three relationships in life, and all, for the believer, are centered in God—the ultimate relationship. I have a relationship to *myself* and to my *neighbor* (all people, not just the folks next door), and I have a relationship to the *world* that my neighbor and I inhabit—the whole world, not just Bartlesville. These relationships are God-centered because Jesus, who is God, centered himself in us—irrational, illogical, but true…and awesome. God, the Creator of all, entered the flesh of a particular person, Jesus, who found himself situated within a particular family, Joseph and Mary, among particular neighbors, Jews and Gentiles, in a real world of the first century (a real, political, social, economic and religious situation within the Roman Empire).

God-in-Christ became incarnate—took flesh in history—entered the human condition. God-in-Christ experienced birth, childhood and family, acceptance and rejection, suffering and death—an ignominious death at that. Incarnation is the mystery in which God truly becomes *human* yet remains totally *other*. We who are the Church—and we *are* the Church. We are the Church who believe in *God*, not merely in Metropolitan Life or in the GNP or in Americanism, or in success, power, or possessing. We believe in God. Believing, remember, is a verb, not a noun. To be in a right relationship with God—to love God, to know God, to be intimate with God—is to be in a right relationship to myself, to my neighbor, and to the world that my neighbor and I inhabit. This includes, of course, Bosnia, Somalia, and Haiti …and the west side of Bartlesville.

I cannot love God abstractly, for God-in-Christ is forever *really present* in *this* world *now*…and I will know and experience and love God within the particular experiences of those relationships. That is, knowing, experiencing, responsibly loving myself; knowing, experiencing, loving particular persons; and loving other things together: the world around us. So our faith, at first blush, must be experienced —incarnational from the bottom up, and not from the top down. We experience faith as the early church did: *within* human events, but we do not, then, set our experiences in concrete, as we assuredly have done.

For example, remembering that faith is a verb, how come I believe that God is a "Trinity"? Is it because some church council in the fourth century decreed it (made belief a noun), or is it because I've come to experience that without community, without intimate, knowing, loving relationships, I cannot be me, and you cannot be fully you; that the glory of God is our humanity fully alive, made in the image and likeness of God who is a community. I've come to know God as Trinity through my real experiences of community. For instance, the family community is basic to experiencing God as Trinity. If I do not, in any way, experience community, I cannot know God as Trinity. I may, of course, know *about* God as Trinity but I will not *know* God as Trinity. I would suspect that most Americans cannot really believe in God as Trinity, except abstractly in some credal statement or catechism answer. Why? Because most Americans are "lone rangers" with our cultural masks. (We don't need Tonto unless to *use* him.) Individualism is the bottom line; "community" has little, if no place in our society, and that's precisely why it is difficult to forge communities even within the Church itself, a Church that claims to be a community.

Historically, our theology has been from the top down, and therefore for the most part has been theoretical and abstract, unwittingly denying the incarnation. In this abstract context, "commitment to Christ and his values" means that Christ becomes an extension of our own culture and values—the American way, Pat Robertson's way. Rather than letting Christ impose himself on us, we have imposed our image onto him (and that, by the way, is why much of our religious art is so bad, so tasteless). This is prob-

> THE GOSPEL DEMANDS MORE FROM US THAN FISH ON FRIDAY, MASS ON SUNDAY AND FULFILLING OUR EASTER DUTY.

ably why the study of Scripture today is a bit scary for us. The gospel demands more from us than fish on Friday, Mass on Sunday and fulfilling our Easter duty.

Jesus takes *flesh* in Word and Sacrament and Community, and calls *us* to *be* his body: to walk the extra mile, turn the other cheek, share the extra shirt or blouse, and to do it with this particular man, this particular homeless woman, this particular hungry child, whether we "like" them or not.

If the Church is to survive as a witness to Christ's values (and not society's conventional wisdom), it will be within small communities. If we are going to commit ourselves to responsible self-love, particularly love of neighbor, and love of other things together, we must prayerfully and consistently reflect on *that commitment* within a community; share our stories, trust our experience. Unfortunately, we have been told *not* to trust our experience. We are evidently, since we are sheep, told to trust only sister, priest or bishop. Without denying those, when they are credible, I believe we can also *listen* to our own experiences within a community of faith—*not just alone*, for a *believing* community will always offer a corrective. In a society of "lone rangers," of rugged individualists, it is difficult to trust the individual experience without the checks and balances of an intimate community. The future of the Church in our society will be found within authentic community, loving God above all things with all our heart, mind and soul; loving our neighbors (*all* neighbors) as we love ourselves; and, at the same time, loving other things together.

Chapter 4 • Community

COMMUNITY LIFE

Acts 2:42–47; John 20:19–31

The first reading is one of Luke's classic summary statements about the life of the primitive community. It was a kind of benign Communist cell. It didn't last too long. With the coming of Constantine, it went by the way. Luke spelled out four of its constituent elements: 1) the apostles' instruction; 2) the community life; 3) the breaking of the bread; and 4) the prayers.

The first, third and fourth elements can all be found in our Eucharistic celebrations today, but the second, "the community life," is too often missing. Its absence makes the other three more difficult, if not impossible, for what else is the Eucharist if not for the building of the Body of Christ? And, how can the Body of Christ *become* the Body of Christ without community?

In the past the church has been, in a sense, like a bunch of bananas—pious bananas, quite a few holy bananas—but remained bananas hanging together from the same stalk, which was Christ, the same source of life, which was Christ, even touching each other inadvertently at times when the pews were full, but rarely, truly conscious of our relationship *to one another, in Christ,* and the responsibilities *that* relationship demands. About the only time, probably, was at Bingo.

In the Gospel account Jesus forgives his disciples and, in turn, demands that they forgive one another, (even gives them the power to do so)! As if to test the extent of their forgiveness, God granted them the opportunity to live with the unbelieving Thomas for a week who stubbornly refuses to cooperate. There is a cartoon that has Peter saying to weeping Thomas, "We're not ashamed of your lack of faith, Thomas. You were just a shade stupider than the rest of us." All of them admitting their limitations and shortcomings.

Just what makes a group, a bunch of bananas, become a *community?* It is what makes true community so attractive to us and yet something that seems to elude us. We seem to be always moving *toward* community and never quite getting there. From time to time we experience it at special moments only to have it conceal itself again behind the busy-ness of every day. Yet this property that attracts us and makes us feel so "at home" is at the same time what we find frightening about community. We are dealing here with a remarkable paradox and mystery of both human and Christian life. Those special moments in which you experience community clearly reveal—and down deep we know it is true—that real community is *not* based on the things we prize *most* about ourselves. Authentic community is not based on our talents, our competence or our strengths; not on our goodness, our virtue or our sinlessness. Paradox of paradoxes, community *is* based on our weakness—our finitude, our inabilities—and even our falls from grace. The mystery can be summed up in the statement: our strengths divide us; it is in our weakness that we are one!

Chapter 4 • Community

Why do we think folks join A.A.? Because of their goodness, because of their strengths, because of their discipline? No, because they are drunks. Why do we join codependency groups? Not because of our strengths but because of our weakness. Why don't we learn this in the Catholic Church? These groups come close to the ideals of community but do not reach it. Such groups allow people to let go of their need to *appear* to be perfect and seamless, and that creates the atmosphere where community is most likely to happen. The work that is ours to do in company with others is not, precisely, the forming of community, but rather what is preliminary to that; the necessarily painful work of unmasking ourselves, so that in the presence of others, the power of our *shared weakness* can transform not only our little group, but hopefully the world around us.

> JESUS IS NOT TEACHING US HOW TO ARM OURSELVES, BUT SOMEHOW TO "DISARM" OURSELVES.

We see Jesus in the Word, the Jesus whom we call our Lord and our God. Like Thomas, this Jesus coming in the midst of us and talking about gentleness, and about poverty of Spirit, about *giving* first of all instead of receiving, about vulnerability, about unconditional openness to the world around us, that may or may not inflict pain. He is not teaching us how to arm ourselves, but somehow to "disarm" ourselves. He is not understood. We thought for sure that the answer was to get this "Christian" thing to work…so we wanted a triumphant religion, and a religion that was "right," and orthodox, that was on top, in control, and had power.

And then this Jesus uses words that somehow upset that spirit: words and images of vulnerability. "A person who loses his life will save it."

Something else is going on here. Something we can't see, maybe something we don't want to see, something maybe we're afraid to see in the culture we live in. And that is, that we have to let go of our desire to win, to be on top, to be always right, to be in control, to use power. What the *world* celebrates as strength is really the most profound kind of impotence. I cannot think of anything stupider than some eastern American Bishops hiring an advertising firm to convince Catholics that abortion is evil. If the Word of God, proclaimed from the pulpit, cannot persuade Catholics of the evil of abortion, what can advertising do? Perhaps we should check out what is being said from the pulpits. Perhaps even check me out. I'm always suspect.

In our troubled days and troubled world, it is vital that we have the opportunities to restore the second constituent element of the Church: "the community life." That is why we changed the name of this parish from the Church of St. James to the Community of St. James—to have a word that says what we should be. Whatever a church is, besides a building, it is vital to gather, to be with those we can trust, and in whose presence we can begin to explore the latent power that lies hidden in our weaknesses and vulnerability—the power of the Holy Spirit which, in our weakness, in our very emptiness, will fill up what is lacking, and bring about—through community—the transformation of the world.

AT THIS TIME

"…in the name of the Father, and of the Son, and of the Holy Spirit."
—Matthew 28:19

We, who believe in God, who is Trinity,
are created
in that image and likeness
summoned in baptism
to transcend
our individualities,
go beyond them
into communities
of knowing and loving
where the many
are becoming one
because *we* are one
for the many
for to deny community
is to deny our very selves
("…love your neighbor
as you love yourself").

EPIPHANY—IMAGINATION

Isaiah 60:1–6; Ephesians 3:2,3,5,6; Matthew 1:1–12

The Rabbi was exceedingly gracious to university deans who visited him, but he would never reply to their questions or be drawn into their theological speculations. To his disciples, who marveled at this, he said, "can one talk about the ocean to a frog in a well, or about the divine to people who are restricted by their concepts?"
—Anthony de Mello

All three readings this morning from this Epiphany feast are about people who could imagine. Imagination is a future-oriented gift, a creative function—the ability to gather and bring together previous knowledge, and project it into the not yet. People working with liturgy reform back in the fifties, prior to Vatican II, imagined a Mass in English. They knew from history that the Mass was in Greek among the Greeks, and then in Latin among the Romans. Why couldn't it be in English among Americans?

Isaiah, Paul and the Magi are all imaginers. They see the present for what it is, but they also see futures in grace-filled visions. The key is *grace-filled* visions. Godless visions can become nightmares, and yet, still be followed. As Herod heard the Magi's story, he began to envision the slaughter of the innocents. Because of the difficulties involved in discerning godly from ungodly visions, we end up putting a damper on *all* imagination. Pretty clear that in our secular

Chapter 4 • Community

society we see great confusion toward creative, yet untried, solutions to vexing problems. We are cautious by nature, tending to tinker with what we know, making some unimaginative adjustments to what is. Politicians excel at this. The "Star Trek" folks may "go boldly where no one has gone before," but our pattern is usually to go exactly where others have gone before. This is readily seen in the church's current failure of imagination. I've heard a rumor that the Cardinal Archbishop of Los Angeles is planning on using a gift of $25 million to build a new cathedral. If so, it reflects no imagination, no vision—simply going where others have gone before: more buildings! And if there is anything we don't need in the Catholic Church, it is more buildings. We have too many now.

When I grew up, in what they call "the good old days," the way you came to be a monsignor was to build a building. Then if the guy who followed you paid off the debt, he also was made a monsignor. No visions! We could not possibly imagine twenty years ago a married clergy, yet we have three married priests right here in our diocese who were former Episcopal or Lutheran clergy. Can we not imagine a married Catholic clergy? I would suggest we had better. If celibacy is more important than Eucharist, then we're in trouble. No imagination. Like Isaiah, Paul and the Magi, John the XXIII, who summoned the Second Vatican Council, was an imaginer, a person of vision, a person of hope. Today, imagination seems to be heresy.

Yet we believe that God *will* make God's will known. God *will* find a messenger. A revelation *will* come. The great prophets, apostles, doctors of the church in the early centuries put their imagination in the service of God. Prayer, in part, could easily be called "imagining with God." Isaiah in exile imagines a renewed future for Jerusalem and a covenant people. The Magi are moved to risk a long journey in search of a newborn Child whose significance surpasses their understanding. Paul imagines a grand, cosmic plan kept secret until revealed in Christ: that all things are being reconciled and brought into unity through Christ Jesus. Risk and resistance in each case were met and overcome. When some of the powers of Rome, back in the sixties, tried to delay his calling the Council, John XXIII called them "prophets of doom" and moved up the date.

God works through imagination. What we cannot imagine, we cannot do. Paul tells us of our free access to God that is built on trust. Trust and imagination have one thing in common: they are not certainties. They are the fuel for taking on and modeling the future with God. Imagination and trust are the ingredients of hope. On a personal level, we have some very practical examples. Praying *for* the sick should include imagining the person as recovered. Persons who cannot *imagine* joy together may never experience it. A community of faith that cannot imagine committed and vigorous ministry to the larger community will never offer it. What is desperately needed, it would seem to me, throughout the faith community and throughout the whole society, is a healing of imagination. Without imagination, without vision, there can be no hope. The

Chapter 4 • Community

Epiphany is *not* about certainties given, but about hopes revealed.

We are Jerusalem and *we* must be a light to the world.

AT THIS TIME

"...we must have the same love for one another."
—1 John 4:11–16

That is, *all* others
   unconditionally.
God is love.
   If we do not abide in love,
   (for *all* others)
   we do not abide in God,
   nor God in us.

GLOBAL VILLAGE

Acts 2:1–11; 1 Corinthians 12:3–7,12,13; John 20:19–23

If we shrink the earth's population to a global village of precisely 100 people, it would look like this:

Of the 100, there would be 57 Asians, 21 Europeans (14 of these from the Western Hemisphere), and 8 Africans; of the 100, there would be 51 females, 49 males; 70 non-white, 30 white; 70 non-Christian, 30 Christian. 50% of the entire world's wealth would be in the hands of 6 people, and all 6 would be citizens of the U.S.; of the 100, 80 would live in substandard housing, 70 would be unable to read, 50 would suffer malnutrition, and 1 would have a college education.

Increasingly, we are coming to understand what it means to live in a global village. Peoples, nations, and cultures that not so long ago were a distant mystery, unteachable and unknowable, are now brought closer and made accessible to us through the development of modern technology.

> WE MUST TAKE THE WORD OUT OF THE DEEP FREEZE AND LET IT SET US ON FIRE.

For some within the church, this is an exciting reality. It provides previously unimagined opportunities for information and understanding. For others, it is a matter of great concern. Having to make one's home within this same global village with people whose thoughts differ; whose mannerisms, habits and lifestyles are other than your own; and whose attitudes toward the Source of Life differ…all of this can be seen as a threat to a uniform understanding of what it means to be the community of God's own.

In an attempt to provide security, the concerned and threatened build barriers to ensure that none of the foreign winds that blow will permeate their own structures within the global village. Rules are set

Chapter 4 • Community

down like fence posts. High-voltage wire encircles their boundaries, jolting those who come too close to the borders from either the inside or the outside. (Catholic theologians summarily are excommunicated without due process; Asian forms of meditation are rejected outright.) Litmus tests, like gates, are put firmly into place. Guards are hired from within to stand watch, allowing only those who have passed the doctrinal and dogmatic security check to enter the precious confines. No one or no thing uninvited is welcome...a policy of exclusion. From the outside it appears that the defense of the concerned and threatened is sure.

On this Sunday (Graduation Sunday), however, the fire of Pentecost burns throughout the global village. Gathering energy from the faithful winds of change, the fire burns with abandon. Through the closed gates of fear, it burns. Through the barricades of the concerned and threatened, it burns. With passion and strength, the tongues of fire burn, bringing to ash the human walls that would protect and separate the concerned and threatened from others within the global village.

A story:

> A white preacher one time visited his black brethren in the same denomination, and shared Sunday worship. Afterwards he shook his head in bewilderment. "I don't understand it," he said. "Compared to your people, my church is a corpse. And yet we preach the same gospel you do; we profess the same creed. I have good people. What makes the difference?" "I'll tell you," said his black

brother. "Our gospel *is* the same but it's like two porterhouse steaks. You keep yours in the deep-freeze. Ours is on fire."

My dear graduates, we must take the Word out of the deep freeze and let it set us on fire. The light of the Pentecost fire is at once exciting and frightening, for it illuminates the reality of a power far greater than all the strategically placed boundaries of a people concerned and threatened. This fire cannot be contained. It cannot be confined. The flames of the Pentecost fire continue to dance through the global village until every heart in the land burns within.

When the smoke of this Pentecost fire clears, all that remains in the global village is the community of God's own and the foundation on which they stand. That foundation is the common ground of holiness and grace. When the sound of the rushing wind dies down, a song of many tongues rises from the circle of burning hearts surrounding the remains of smoldering fence posts and gates. Many tongues.

Many gifts. Many signs and wonders. We do not fear. We are not afraid. For it is one God, one Spirit in Christ who creates and renews the face of the global village, which is indeed the community of God's very own.

Chapter 4 • Community

FEAST OF THE IMMACULATE CONCEPTION

Luke 1:26–38

An angel was sent from God to a town in Washington County called Bartlesville, to a Community of faith named St. James. The angel said, "Rejoice, so highly favored ones, the Lord is with you and blessed are you among peoples." The people of St. James were deeply troubled by his words and wondered what his greeting meant.

The angel went on to say, "Do not fear, people of St. James, you have found favor with God. Through Baptism and the Eucharist and the Word, you have conceived and borne a presence whose name is Jesus. In you his dignity will be great and through you he will be the Lord of all."

But the Community of St. James cried, "How can this be? Why us? Whom do we know?"

The angel answered, "The Holy Spirit has come upon you and the power of the Most High has overshadowed you, hence, the holy offspring to be born will be called the Body of Christ, the People of God.

"You may consider yourselves to be fruitless, but nothing is impossible with God."

The Community said, "We are the servants of the Lord, let it be done to us as you say."

With that, the angel left.

Chapter 5

BEING CHURCH

WE SAY, "WE SEE"

We say, "we see,"
but we do not see,
and our sin remains.

And how will the world
know we are "from God,"
if we look like
we are from the world?

And how did we manage
to make Christ a king
when Jesus aspired
to servanthood?

And if Jesus is servant,
how did his "low church"
become the "high church"?

And, speaking
of "high church,"
how can we march
twenty robed singers,
two robed servers,
one robed deacon,
and three robed priests
in a procession
to Calvary
where Jesus
was dis-robed?

We say, "we see,"
but we do not see
and our sin remains.

And how can the Church
be influential
in the world
when she herself
is affluential
before the world?

And why does the Church
serve the rich first
and the poor second
when Jesus claimed
that the second
shall be first
and the first second,
or, maybe, even last?

And how can we say
"we care for the poor,"
when we vote
with the rich
to keep the poor, poor,
and so,
our sin remains
as "we care for the poor."

And when will the Church become
as financially insecure
as the poor
she says she serves,
and how can the Church

be financially secure
when Jesus
had no place to lay his head?

We say, "we see,"
but we do not see,
and our sin remains.

And how will others
come to see
and believe
if we have egg
on our face,
instead of mud
in our eye?

And how can the Church
open the eyes of the world
to its injustice
when she is blind
to her own:
with her unilateral decisions,
without concern for,
without consultation with
the very members
of Christ's Body
for whom she is deciding?

We say, "we see,"
but we do not see,
and our sin remains.

And how can the Church
be prophetic:
A sign of the kingdom

to the secular world,
when she seems,
at times,
to be in the world
and of it?

And how can the Church
be prophetic
to corporations
when the corporate Church
is run like a business
and not like
who it is:
the Body of Christ?

And how can the Church
be prophetic
in the presence of government
when the present government
is spending for war
and not for the poor,
and when the Church herself
gives preference to power,
knowing full well,
that Jesus heard only
the cries of the poor?

We say, "we see,"
but we do not see,
and our sin remains.

And how will
a world in darkness
experience us

as children of light
when we appear to be
awake to apathy
and asleep to empathy?

And when we ask the world
with our very lives,
"Do you believe
in the Son of Man?"
the world will respond,
"Who is he
that we might believe?"
And we, the Church,
must answer:
"You have seen him,
he is speaking to you now."

CHRIST'S PRESENCE
Matthew 13:1–23

I was born in New York City. I was raised in Los Angeles and spent my young adult life in Tulsa, Oklahoma. For a city boy like me, it has always been a struggle to explain the agricultural customs of Jesus' time so that my hearers would have a better understanding of why this careless farmer did not plant with greater care. It is easier today because gardening experts have been advocating a return to a method of planting that goes back to the "old ways." In wide-row gardening, the planting is done by scattering the seeds over the bed and then raking it in: a far cry from the careful rows of evenly placed seeds most of us were taught to construct. It would seem that the "row" method allows much more *control* over the result—or so we think.

Inevitably, as in the parable, some seeds will fail to germinate, others sprout and will be plucked by crows, and there will be gaps in the carefully planned row. Still, we would really like to think that we can control the end result of our labors. Perhaps this is why the traditional interpretation of the parable, from the Matthian community, is so appealing. If we were to use more effort, more care, and try very hard *not* to be *those* shallow people in whom the Word does not thrive, God will make *our* lives fruitful. The idea speaks to our cultural values and makes sense to us. It is what I call *boot-strap piety*, part of our rugged individualistic spirit in this country. However, in this parable, the heedless sower receives a reward far beyond his imagination. Even if he didn't know any better, such methods should not have such an enormous reward! Given what everyone knows about the risks of farming, the parable says, there is no way the sower can take credit for the outcome. God gives the harvest and more abundantly than we deserve or can possibly imagine. It is up to us then, to take that parable and talk about its meaning in our lives—not what it meant to Jesus, not what it meant to the Matthian community—what does it mean now? That could be a subject for a marvelous retreat.

> THE WORD TELLS US THAT GOD IS NOT BOUND BY OUR MEAGER EXPECTATIONS.

In the midst of things we cannot control, and in spite of our struggle to deal with uncertain outcomes, the Word tells us that God is not bound by our meager expectations. Even when things seem unpromising, the Word says we can trust God to safeguard the future, to bring not just a good outcome but a better one that we can envision. This parable is all *too* often used for the wrong reasons, about the *kinds* of Christians we may find in our congregations or what we will discover when we look within ourselves: hard ground, thorns, shallow soil. It has been used to justify writing off those who are less zealous than the prevailing standard, those who lose their way for a time, or fail to live up to the group's expectations: like many young people who leave the church may be looked upon then as "the thorns." We no longer need to pay attention to them in their direction. Some Catholics purse up their lips looking like they were sucking persimmons, staring down at those people whom we have written off.

Yet, all of us, at various times in our lives, are all of those things; that is the truth of the matter. Most of us have experienced days in which the Word has had a hard time penetrating our thick defenses, and then suddenly grace breaks through. Jesus knew all of that, of course. That is why he told this story of the way in which God provides abundantly for us. We do have a choice and we make it daily. We can live as the sower did, flinging ourselves into life with some abandon (though most of us can't manage much abandon) and trust that God will redeem our foolishness, bless our more promising efforts, and bring out of it all a blessing that is beyond human reason. Or we can, and often do, live very carefully, trying to avoid mistakes, risking a little, but not too much; in short, living as though we were in this alone. It is a lonely business to live like that, trying to control the uncontrollable thing that is life. Even then, God has promised that all will be redeemed. The Word will not be made void but will achieve its end. Jesus invites us to *live* in that promise *now*.

The Christ Presence *is* among us (Eucharist, Word, Community) urging us to re-interpret the Word and *live* it.

That Word, seeded in us, is the hope of the world. The parable tells us:

We *can* eliminate war and bring about a peaceful world.

We *can* realize a family of humankind living in harmony with one another.

We *can* eliminate hunger.

We *can* educate all our children.

We *can* affirm the divine presence in *every* life, that we may share in the glorious freedom of the children of God *if we live in that promise now.*

We *can*!

PERSONAL JOURNEYS

Matthew 2:1–12

There is an ancient legend, which Father John Shea shares in one of his books, that says the Magi were three different ages. The story goes like this: Gaspar was a young man, Balthazar in his middle years and Melchior a senior citizen. When they approached the stable at Bethlehem, they first went in *one at a time.* Melchior found an old man like himself with whom he was quickly at home. They spoke together of memory and gratitude. The middle-aged Balthazar encountered a teacher of his own age. They talked passionately of leadership and responsibility. When young Gaspar entered, a young prophet meets him with words of reform and promise.

The three met outside the stable and marveled at how each had gone in to see a newborn child, but each had met someone of his own years. They gathered their gifts in their arms and entered *together* a second time. In a manger on a bed of straw was a child twelve days old.

The message of Christ, his Word, talks to every stage of the life process…and its passages. The old hear the call to integrity and wisdom. The middle-aged hear the call to generativity and responsibility. The young hear the call to identity and intimacy.

The Word of revelation accompanies us on our own personal journeys. We marvel at the richness and adaptability of the Word. To find Christ at any stage in our lives is to find ourselves. Yet, when all enter together—the young, the middle-aged, and the old—we find a deeper truth. No matter where we are in the life process, we are still and always, *children* of God. Scripture never speaks of the adults of God, it always refers to us as the children of God. So childlike we must always be in the life's process. Every day when our feet "hit the deck," it is a new way of discovering God's presence in our lives. Our dependency, our indebtedness, does not go away with maturity.

> WE MARVEL AT THE RICHNESS AND ADAPTABILITY OF THE WORD.

So there are many stages in the life of a human person and each stage presents different struggles and different opportunities. Yet, at each stage there remains the child in us. When we go in separately, we know we are in different places and different times. When we go in together, as a community, we know that even though we are different, we are the same.

G. K. Chesterton, the wonderful Catholic poet of the early part of this century, ends his poem, "The House of Christmas," like this:

> To an open house in the evening
>   home shall people come.
> To an older place than Eden
>   and a taller town than Rome.
> To the end of the way
>   of the wandering star
> To the things that cannot be
>   and that are.
> To the place where God is homeless
>   and all people are at home.

AT THIS TIME

"…called to be an apostle…"
—ROMANS 1:1–7

Called
  …to be sent;
set apart
  …to be in touch;
powerless
  …to be strong;
quiet
  …to proclaim.

This is how
the birth of Christ…
comes about in me.

REAL LIFE

Luke 15:1–3,11–32

The parable is about hitting bottom and surviving. Hitting bottom is not the same as thinking about it or feeling something about it. Hitting bottom is hitting bottom. Not everyone who experiences it survives and not *all* survival leads to a new life, to what Paul calls a new creation. The parable tells us about an unusual kind of survival. The prodigal son does not survive by pulling himself by the bootstraps. He is not a prototype for the American capitalist. Nor does he get out of a tight spot by shrewdly exploiting his father's soft-heartedness. This is not a story of a will-power decision—a decision to clean up his act. It is not about making resolutions like those we make when we are fat and out of shape.

Listen to him: "I will arise and go to my Father." This is the voice of a poor and deeply wounded human being whose life has failed, and failed utterly. The prodigal son is a good-for-nothing spendthrift. A wastrel and a fool who *returns home* empty handed because there is no where else to go! He is a wreck, and no innocent lamb. Both he and his elder brother *know* he deserves all the misery he has. He truly brought it upon himself.

Nevertheless—and this never-the-less is at the heart of the whole story—he simply gets up and returns to the one who used to love him, and still does. And that's tough! *Hard!* To return to those who know and love us *after* we have sinned is the hardest journey in the world. Especially if we have sinned bravely with flair and dash in a big, dramatic, public and excruciatingly visible way like the prodigal. He did it with gusto, like Martin Luther taught: "If you are going to sin, sin lustily!"

But, of course, most of us don't have to worry about returning home after sinning like that because we don't have such dramatic sins. Our sins are often smalltime and boring just like the smalltime Lenten resolutions we design to fix them up. Perhaps you and I sin so little because we love so little. How can we sin big unless we really get involved with people. Do we think that "loose living" means just throwing money around or wasting time and talent? *Real sin* involves *real* life, and *real* life involves *real* people and *real* intimate and responsible relationships. Some of us here may be so removed from each other, so poor as persons, that we can't even *feel* our sins decently. How can we experience sin as a *death* in our lives when we are barely alive in the first place, drudging along without love or life? Believe me, I understand this quite well.

In the late '60s and early '70s, most of my priest friends became deeply involved—intimate in the lives of real people. The involvement eventually led them *out* of the priesthood and *into* marriage—no hanky-panky here, but risk! Responsible, serious, loving relationships. Intimacy may lead to sexual celebration but not necessarily. However, sexual action without intimacy is manipulative and exploitative.

We need to face up to the real poverty of spiritless lives: to wasteful indulgences (the mega hours of

TV watching), to our decadence as citizens in a soft-bellied, short-sighted, stingy nation. We are even poorer than the prodigal son because we refuse to acknowledge the bottom that is all around us.

Who is poorer than the over-fed rich who no longer even know their *love* is dead? Who can be further from the gospel than those who no longer know their *need* of God? And tragically it is quite often the super-*religious* folks who no longer know that need. Is there anyone poor enough among us—simple enough, needy enough, sinful enough—to be able to appreciate the taste of love that is like manna in the desert? Anyone who needs love so badly they would take even its scraps under the table, like the younger son?

> WHO CAN BE FURTHER FROM THE GOSPEL THAN THOSE WHO NO LONGER KNOW THEIR NEED OF GOD?

And what sort of love was it that filled the *father's* heart? Was it a love that knows how much it *is* loved and is ready to give all it has again and again and again? A person who thought he loved *too little* because he was loved *so much?*

Who of us will *love* this way?

Who will let the Spirit of God's love poured into us take over and fill up the life we share together as Christ's poor, and as sinners who share Christ's meal —fill us *so much* that it spills out of us and into the world like a banquet for the starving? Who among us will do that?

BEING OURSELVES WITH GOD

Isaiah 6:1,2,3–8; 1 Corinthians 15:1–11; Luke 5:1–11

My sister, Pat, mother of twelve, told me the story one time of my five-year-old grand-nephew, facing a dilemma. How could he get rid of the mosquitoes that plagued him and his friends? He sat and pondered for a while until his mother, my niece—worried by the quiet—asked what was the matter.

He looked up and said, "Do you think it would be all right to ask God to take all the mosquitoes and make them fly higher and higher until they got lost?" My niece, with the infinite wisdom of a parent, responded, "Yes, I think you could ask God for that." When she returned a little later, however, she was surprised to find her son still silently rooted. Once again she asked, "What's the matter?" My grand-nephew replied, "Mommy, what is God's telephone number?"

That perhaps, for many of us, is the problem in our relationship with God. God has an unlisted number. No matter how much we seek, we do not find; no matter how much we call, there is no answer. God is silent, distant, perhaps on vacation.

But, then again, perhaps our real problem is the fact that we have forgotten that God has *already* called and is *still* calling us. He is still hanging, hopefully, on the line.

The essence of Christianity is not *our initiative* but *our response* to God's initiative. Have we so radi-

Chapter 5 • Being Church

cally lost touch with our roots, so fully reversed the essence of Christianity? Is God at our beck and call (some would seem to have it that way)—or are we at God's beck and call?

There are two areas that merit attention: clutter and fear. In every part of society, rural and urban, the activities may change but not the *clutter*. This frenetic multiplication of tasks does not allow us to remember *ourselves*, let alone God. We are so busy doing things that we become things, instruments for the maintenance of society —ciphers—coming and going.

Until we are willing to find a space, a time within which we can *listen*, we prevent ourselves from hearing the call that lies at the very root of ourselves: the call of God, who invites us to be simply ourselves. Lent is a special season for listening, for becoming ourselves-in-Christ.

> THE ESSENCE OF CHRISTIANITY IS NOT OUR *INITIATIVE* BUT OUR *RESPONSE* TO GOD'S INITIATIVE.

But suppose we do break through? Suppose we overcome the tendencies of our age to make us over into objects, and begin to hear the call of God? Then, too often, fear takes over and deafens us. Like Peter, I'm all too familiar with false starts. I've tried to be whole, to be good, to be courageous. I've gone fishing before for integrity, honesty, patience, gentleness…and I've come up empty.

I'm too down and out to believe that I'm capable of being whole, alive, engaged, creative—or, on another tack, I'm too far gone. I enjoy my prejudices. (Depart from me for I am a sinful man, O Lord!) I'm not fit to be a live, creative, loving person, and so I shout, "Get away from me! Go away." Like Peter, I say to myself, "It is not good to be *too* near to God. God wants too much. God knows too much. God is too single-minded. Who wants to be with Jesus? Who wants to open his or her heart to God that much? Who wants to be reached—touched?"

Because to be touched means to be *sent* to walk the path of integrity that we might become whole *in God*. To do less is self-destructive, to drown ourselves in the sea of forgetfulness, to be snagged by insipid piety—which turns us into disposable objects to be used and cast away.

This Lent we need to break through the clutter of our lives, dare to overcome the fear and be *still* enough to hear the voice of God. Hearing it, we can become who we are: prophets and apostles proclaiming resurrection and hope to a world that has too often forgotten and that is too often afraid.

SEND ME

Isaiah 6:1–8; 1 Corinthians 15:1–11; Luke 5:1–11

Simon already had a job when he encountered Jesus in Luke's Gospel. He wasn't doing very well at it. People in his day who depended on fishing for a livelihood, and people

Chapter 5 • Being Church

who rely on it now, have no control over the availability of the product. On a day when the fish weren't biting, there was nothing to do but sit around on the beach mending nets and complaining about the economy. Simon was under-employed.

Paul, on the other hand, was over-employed when he met the Risen Christ on that famous journey to Damascus. He was extremely busy—no time to think, no chance to really evaluate what he was doing. Night and day, he was caught up in the demands of a growing business: bounty-hunting for the Pharisees. Running down Christians like a western posse—a task that kept him going beyond the limits of endurance because he was so sure of the rightness of his efforts.

Isaiah may well have been the sort of son who drove his parents mad. He was a day-dreamer with no clear career objectives, and worse still, he wrote poetry. At least he liked to hang around the temple; surely he would stay out of trouble.

All three figures had far too much on their minds to be bothered with the question of vocation. Parenthetically, by vocation, we are not talking about *choice* of careers, or limiting the word to what it used to mean. When I grew up Catholic, vocation evidently meant either the seminary or the nunnery. I often thought that was funny that priests and nuns had vocations and everybody else had careers. We see how absurd we can be at times. By vocation in this context, we are speaking about how each one of us responds to God's presence and call in our lives—

regardless of careers. (Vocation comes from the Latin word *vocare*, meaning "to call.")

Simon and Paul were simply doing what had to be done; Isaiah was wrapped up in a world of his own. It took something extraordinary to catch their attention.

Jesus joins the fishing expedition, and Simon becomes weak in the knees. Paul on the road to Damascus hears Jesus rebuking him in the midst of a flashing light, and no longer sees what he saw before. Isaiah hears the voice of the Lord, and the whole earth trembles. All three react, first by expressing their own unworthiness, and then by turning their lives around and never looking back.

In the Epiphany season we emphasize God's appearances at Jesus' birth and at his baptism, sometimes viewing them as unrelated to the way we go about our business of life. *These* three stories remind us that epiphanies (manifestations of Christ's presence) may come in the middle of workdays, like Peter, to people who aren't looking for anything different, like Isaiah, and who may not welcome the interruption, like Paul. They show us that epiphany has to do with vocation (or call), that the uncovering of God's character before our very eyes confronts us and turns us around. Such a confrontation makes it impossible to resist our vocation, even when it means suffering, wrenching change and a new identity.

The confrontations may not be quite as spectacular as these three, and we may not be up to discerning them. For lack of reflective prayer, we may not be open to the Spirit's call at all. Through prayer—I am

Chapter 5 • Being Church

talking about reflective prayer, quiet prayer—we momentarily leave the shallows of merely doing and enter the deeper waters of being, that is, of being who we really are, who we are *called* to be: the body and blood of Jesus in *our* world, *wherever* we are. In turn, we learn to read the world and read the Word; to see more clearly what our values are and what we need to be and do.

And suddenly, like Simon, we are astounded. We can no longer pull fish out of the water to die; we are called to pull people out of the water to live. It appears to me that a lot of people in our society are drowning, rich and poor, but for different reasons.

In sacred places, like Isaiah; where we work, like Peter; on the road, like Paul, meeting God demands change. Moses was called from being an overseer of Hebrew slaves to lead his people to freedom. Zacchaeus, upon meeting Jesus, changed from being a cheat and coming down from his tree, to become an honest and generous man. Saul, the persecutor of Christians, became Paul the Apostle of Jesus. And the young Isaiah was changed from the comfortable aristocrat to the fiery prophet of God…still writing poetry. They all felt totally inadequate, but with the calling comes power. Even in an old fishing boat,

> WE CAN NO LONGER PULL FISH OUT OF THE WATER TO DIE; WE ARE CALLED TO PULL PEOPLE OUT OF THE WATER TO LIVE.

Jesus had the power to make something new and life-giving out of Simon Peter, the fisherman.

We live in a troubled world—we are all conscious of that—more trouble than I have experienced in my lifetime. A serious and certain madness seems to be present. We have, sadly enough, surrendered the public domain to the secular, value-free professionals. *The world out there needs another Presence.*

Perhaps the words of Isaiah this morning fit each one of us, "Then I heard the voice of the Lord saying, 'Whom shall I send? Who will go for us?' 'Here I am,' I said. 'Send me!'"

Chapter 6

SUFFERING

THEN & NOW

I have come to rate all as lost in the light of the surpassing knowledge of my Lord Jesus Christ.	I have come to rate all as won in the light of my surpassing knowledge of stocks and bonds.

For His sake
I have forfeited everything;
I have accounted all else
rubbish
so that Christ
may be my wealth
and I may be
in Him.

For my own sake
I have forfeited nothing;
I have accounted all
as goodies
so that the world
may be my wealth
and I may be
in it and of it.

The justice I possess
is that which comes
through faith in Christ;
it has its origin
in God
and is based on faith.

The justice I possess
is that which comes
through faith in power;
it has its origin
in ambition
and is based on greed.

I wish to know Christ
and the power flowing
from his resurrection;
likewise to know
how to share
in His sufferings
by being formed
into the pattern
of His death.

I wish to know the world
and power flowing
from its dying.
I do not wish
to know Christ,
nor share in His suffering,
but rather to be formed
into the pattern and lifestyle
of the rich and famous.

Thus do I hope
that I may arrive at
resurrection from the dead.

Thus do I hope
that I have it all now,
not later.

PHILIPPIANS 3:8–14

MAKING CHOICES
Isaiah 45:1,4–6; Matthew 22:15–21

The disciples would frequently be absorbed in questions of right and wrong. Sometimes the answer would be evident enough. Sometimes it was elusive. The Master, if he happened to be present at such discussions, would take no part in them. Once he was confronted with this question: "Is it right to kill someone who seeks to kill me? Or is it wrong?" He said, "How should I know?" The shocked disciples answered, "Then how would we tell right from wrong?" The Master said, "While alive, be dead to yourself, die to yourself. Then act as you will and your action will be right."

—Anthony de Mello

A question that has been constantly asked down through the ages is, what part does God play in the bad things that happen in our world? As we know, the early Hebrews ascribed good and bad alike to God. Later, after their exile in Babylonia, the world of evil was shifted away from God and given over to the hands of Satan or demons. Even today, the TV comedian can assert, "The devil made me do it."

The reading today from Isaiah comes from a time in which there were few scientific explanations for disease or the operation of the universe. People had limited ability to understand what was happening in the world around them.

Today, we need to be able to explain things that happen to us. We need to sense the presence of some order in the world. The absence of explanations produces a level of anxiety that is beyond the tolerance of most of us. Today's Isaian text reassured the anxious Old Testament multitudes that their not-always-friendly world was at least under the control of Someone, and not simply the setting for a series of whimsical events. The text told them that God was in control even to the extent of guiding the actions of people who did not know this God of Israel. The text reassured them that God was the author of all.

> GOD HAS GIVEN US THE RESPONSIBILITY FOR OUR CHOICES.

In the years since the prophets we have come to understand something of the way in which our universe works; some of the mechanics of disease, for example. We know that God does not make us sick as a punishment for sin. Or do we? The Pharisees thought so. The leper was looked upon as one who sinned or he wouldn't have leprosy. Are we still thinking that way? "What did I do to deserve this?" still rings out and challenges what science says about the causes of disease. I suspect that quite often we are so preoccupied with guilt, shame and feelings of unworthiness that we feel we *should be* punished. When we become ill, we assume at a feeling level, that God, who knows about all those "hidden sins," is seeking restitution—that our illness is penance for our misdeeds. So our Simon

Chapter 6 • Suffering

Ligree God wrings his hands. Heh, heh, heh! Perhaps we even hope that we will be absolved through our suffering. If you want to live in that world with that God, God bless you.

As we move to the Gospel, perhaps we can hear the words, "Give to Caesar what is Caesar's, but give to God what is God's," in a slightly different way. Maybe we need to be reminded not to attribute to God that which is not attributable to God. When the Isaian text tells us that God is the author of all, perhaps we can attribute to God what rightly belongs there, by recognizing that God created the possibility for both right and wrong in those made in God's image. That possibility requires that we make choices, and that those choices determine what happens in our lives and the lives of those around us. Bad things happen to us because of a bad choice, or because our physical environment has acted on us, not because God has punished us, or because some evil power has made the thing happen. I remember years ago a book called *The Exorcist* by William Blatty. It was made into a movie; people thronged to it. It was a predecessor to Stephen King. William Blatty made a remark publicly, at the time, that when some avalanches following an earthquake covered some towns in Peru, it was the devil up there on the mountain shoving it over. God has given us the responsibility for our choices. We cannot give that responsibility back to its donor. To accept the responsibility for our choices and exercise the freedom God has given us does not diminish God's power; it simply and wonderfully acknowledges the divine love in its fullest expression.

This reminds me of an old story about the sheep who found a hole in the fence and crept through it. He wandered far and lost his way back. Then he realized he was being followed by a wolf. He ran and ran but the wolf kept chasing him until the shepherd came and rescued him and carried him lovingly back to the fold. In spite of everyone's urgings to the contrary, the shepherd refused to nail up the hole in the fence.

Though we may make the wrong choices, our God is a God of love and mercy. Let us, therefore, risk the anxiety of our own choices, and not render unto God that which belongs to us. While we live, we die to ourselves—as Jesus did. *Then* when we act as we will, our actions will be right.

AT THIS TIME

"Anyone…who aspires to greatness must serve the rest."
—Mark 10:42–45

We find light
   through the darkness
   of affliction.
We find strength
   through the power
   of weakness.
We find greatness
   through the authority
   of service.

Chapter 6 • Suffering

A JOURNEY TOWARD SUFFERING

Mark 8:31

Jesus' suffering, death and resurrection are *faith* events—not to be proved. Jesus suffered, died and was raised from death. This is the bedrock of faith; without either, we are still in our sins.

Suffering, death, resurrection—a paradox, a seeming contradiction. Perhaps the relationship can best be expressed through the analogy of nature. *Out of* winter comes spring—no spring, no winter. Spring does not simply *follow* winter—it organically comes *out of* winter. Within the darkness of winter's womb, spring prepares for birth. Or, for example, a caterpillar dies to being a caterpillar in order to become a butterfly. Wouldn't that be an incredible experience! To go to sleep as a caterpillar and wake up as a butterfly. Paradox: "Whoever saves his life will lose it, but whoever loses his life will find it." Out of loss comes discovery.

We are now journeying to Jerusalem, preparing for and moving toward the three greatest feasts in the church year: Holy Thursday, Good Friday, Easter Sunday. *Thursday:* The Last Supper—a celebration with his friends of a reality that had *already* been going on for years. His life poured out for them, his being broken for them. Paradox: Bread cannot be shared unless it is broken. Wine cannot be shared unless it is poured out. *Good Friday:* The ultimate brokenness—

his death for us. And *out of* his death comes life—the most incredible paradox: Easter Sunday. Without Good Friday there would be no Easter Sunday. There could have been a *Friday* without an Easter Sunday, but it wouldn't have been *Good*. Without a life spent for others, without a life being broken for others, without a life being poured out for others, there would have been no *saving* Good Friday. Jesus' suffering and death was a summing-up, an accumulative finalization of the many dyings in his life. In a real sense, Jesus was already dead when he died—dead, that is, to himself. Instead of dying dead, he died alive. Jesus didn't practice what he preached, he preached what he practiced. He was his Word, his Word was him. "Whoever would save his life will lose it, but whoever loses his life will find it." Jesus spent his entire life losing it for the sake of others, and the "bottom line" was resurrection.

> OUT OF JESUS' DEATH COMES LIFE—THE MOST INCREDIBLE PARADOX.

A correlative paradox is this: Jesus' real birthday was not Christmas. His real birthday was Easter Sunday. On Christmas, God experienced a human-coming-to-be, a dying to divinity, a total immersion into our humanity and its attendant confusion, ambiguity, and suffering. Jesus' humanity, *through* and *out of* his suffering and death, was born into the fullness of life with his Father. Humankind, from the very beginning, decided to save itself. That's sin. Jesus, from the very beginning decided *not* to save himself.

Chapter 6 • Suffering

That's grace. And he, therefore, as man, became Savior, because in losing himself for others, he found himself, on Easter morning, as Son of God and Lord of the universe.

Now that's all well and good, but what does that mean for us here and now? "The Son of Man had to suffer much…" In Baptism, we were immersed—as God became immersed in humanity; we were plunged into Christ's risen humanity, and into his suffering, death and resurrection. If Jesus truly lives, and we believe that he does, then we cannot separate his person from the events of his life. Jesus is always present in the mystery of his suffering, death and resurrection. As someone said, "Jesus is in agony until the end of time."

Our Baptism was our Christmas feast. Inspirited by Jesus' Spirit, we began our personal journey to the Father, in Christ—that is, in the context of the Christian Community, which *is* the Body of Christ. As persons of faith, when we die (our Easter feast) we should already be dead—dead to ourselves, but alive in Christ for others. We should not die dead, but die alive. Like Paul (2 Corinthians 4:6–14), death should be at work in us, but life in our family and in the community where we reside. *To live* paradoxically involves a life-long process of dying and coming to life. Suffering, death and resurrection is happening to us every moment of our lives *if* our relationships are lovingly and responsibly managed. Resurrection then, is not just an intellectual promise, nor just a historical event, but rather a daily experience for us who know that our faith lies not only in remembering, but in living, here and now, *that* memory.

Just recall, for the moment, those times in which we have felt enlarged—or the times in which our lives have been deepened because of what somebody else has meant to us. We locate the *resurrection experience* in our own lives by identifying those moments in which we have become *more of ourselves.* They are almost always related to the action of someone who has loved us enough to make the power of resurrection a reality in our lives. This is not an analogy, but a reality. For example, somebody else trusts us—allowing us to find our own way for the first time. That's resurrection! Somebody, sometimes a stranger, responds to us with a genuine understanding of us and some trial we may be experiencing—and seeing into our lives, that person helps us to see more of ourselves at the same time. That's resurrection! Someone enlarges our lives by honestly letting us see into his or her own life—like a poet, a novelist, or a friend. Someone inspires us to become more ourselves. Who is it in your life? And why is it that he or she gives you courage and strength to keep going, or keep trying to do better?

Now let me turn a moment to the question of *our* resurrecting *others.* The first lesson is that to enlarge the life of another person, we must allow some of our own life to get out. We must let others into our personalities—make room for them in that inner space which we can so jealously keep very much to ourselves. If we are to make the lives of others fuller, we begin by relearning the lessons of suffering and

Chapter 6 • Suffering

dying. Something in us must die if something of the power of our own life is going to get out to transform the suffering and hopelessness of another. It is my own person—*me*—that must be broken, poured out, spent for others. As Christians there is *no other way* to hand over our own spirit if we do not learn to make those small surrenders that put an end to our selfishness.

Small wonder that our society is so alienated. The words of Jeremiah are appropriate for our time, especially for us Christians. We are so sucked in to the values of the world, that we, like the dummies of Jeremiah's day, have created out of the past a presently unjust society, and certainly a fearful future for our children. Jeremiah's people cried, "What is our crime?" The Lord's answer: "Your fathers have forsaken me and followed strange gods, and my law you have not observed." And the gods we follow? The gods of secular humanism, rugged individualism, consumerism and plain old greed.

> LISTENING WELL REQUIRES US TO DIE TO OUR OWN NEEDS AND CURIOSITY.

Let me begin to wind up by exploring a few human ways through which the spirit, or life, makes passage, or is given over from one person to another. Sometimes it is as simple as giving up our own daydreams and pre-occupations, in order that we may pay attention to others…listen to them. The surrender of our *distractions* (which are many) enables us to move closer to others. Apply that to the diarrhea of sports programming on television—no time left to listen to anyone, is there? Listening well requires us to die to our own needs and curiosity, to give up what we wish to speak about so that we can truly hear the message another person wants to give. In other words, *shut up* once in a while! Being with others—making ourselves consciously present to them—requires a death to our own feelings. It's not a question of just being "interested," as we might be in cocktail conversation, but rather of truly being present… *there* for them with compassion.

> PERFECTION HAS NEVER BEEN A REQUIREMENT FOR LOVING.

Finally, all this can be done without our becoming perfect. Even the most flawed of us can still give life to others. Perfection has never been a requirement for loving. Furthermore, we can be a saving people without giving up our own individuality, interests, or lives. Enlarging the lives of others does not demand that we leave no time for ourselves or our families. Enlarging the lives of others only asks that we be willing to pull away from these personal interests at times in order to share our own strength with those who need it. When we give life, we do it in simple exchanges that are so remarkable that we sometimes do not recognize them: in listening to the troubled, in standing with the oppressed, or in winking at a homely girl. This is the way we give life as Jesus did and does, and prepare now for the time when we can fully enter into his resurrection.

Chapter 6 • Suffering

TO DANCE WITH A CROSS

Isaiah 40:1–5,9–11; 2 Peter 3:8–14; Mark 1:1–8

I once asked a group of young children to tell me about John the Baptizer. One little girl, disgust controlling her face, said, "He's the one who ate bugs!" Now, we hope that John's legacy to us is a little loftier than that. But Mark gives us such striking personal detail, not simply to provide something picturesque within the prophetic, but because the bug-eater is meant to be good news, precisely because of his humanness. The voice sent to cry in the wilderness is not a disembodied voice. It is a *human* voice—the eternal Word finding expression in and through our humanity. To prepare the way for the incarnation—God's birth in Christ—God chooses real people who require food (however exotic), clothing, shelter, companionship. God's people are expected to have real needs, appetites and desires. God chooses us *as we are* with all the complexities of our varied personalities, all that it means to be human, to prepare God's way.

We should really change the wording in the song we sing at the end of the preface, to read, "Blessed are *they* who come in the name of the Lord." That "he" in the song is now *us*. God chooses us in our mortality—calls us to speak the Word. God has us frail ones go into the wilderness *out there*, the wasteland of greed and power oppression, in order that God might meet us in *our* wilderness, in the hardness and the desolation and the dryness of ourselves. It is in our very mortality, amid our frailty that God speaks the Word to us. God's way is in and through the wilderness, the struggles, the desert of uncertainties. It is not a way of *our* choosing or a place where we might otherwise want to be. We are not speaking here of power and majesty. The power of God is the folly of the cross: "God chose what is foolish in the world to shame the strong."

We are called to be, like the Israel of the first century, suffering servants. We need not carve new crosses, clothe ourselves with camel hair and eat bugs for little Jesus' sake. The cross is all around us in this mad world we facetiously call "civilization." The cross is with us in the challenge to live the Word more fully, *in* the world but not *of* it. We need to hear God's voice; we need to *be* that voice, reminding ourselves of mortality, calling to repentance, offering tender consolation. It is the work of the wilderness, of the desert times of our lives, that enables us to hear and speak such words. (If we have not comforted, how can we comfort?) Our journey into and through the wilderness prepares the way for God, prepares us for God. The Word we hear in this wilderness is a word of hope and promise; it reminds us that our mortality is not the most important thing about us, and invites us patiently to prepare *now* for the creation of new heavens and a new earth where we will be at home.

> THE WORD WE HEAR IN THIS WILDERNESS IS A WORD OF HOPE AND PROMISE.

Given our destiny then, we should be fully, gloriously human, *capable* of imagining a radically different world... *willing* to journey into the wilderness to meet the God who promises such a world, *faithful* in inviting and sustaining others on the journey, *working* to prepare the way.

What keeps us from despair, what keeps us a people of hope is the Christian paradox: He who is to come is already here. He is in our midst within this community, in our hearts, through Word and Sacrament. That is why, within our very frailty, we can do the unimaginable: We can *dance* down the road with a cross on our back.

AT THIS TIME

"I have witnessed the affliction of my people..."
—Exodus 3:1–8,13–15

The Spirit
comes to us
as fire flaming
within; our hearts,
though on fire,
are never consumed
because the God Who Is
is with us
and sends us
to rescue
the Lord's afflicted
and suffering.

TRIUMPH OF THE CROSS

Numbers 21:4–9; Philippians 2:6–11; John 3:13–17

Growing up Catholic back in the so-called "good old days," much was made of the difference between crosses and crucifixes. The plain cross lacking a corpus was Protestant; the crucifix was Catholic. The two symbolic approaches reflected, at least in theory, two distinct theologies. The Protestant reformers stressed the otherworldly nature of salvation—known, and entered into by faith alone. Rome insisted that this same salvation was accomplished through the humanity of Jesus Christ. Today, believers on both sides are rediscovering the priority of truths they share. Salvation is entirely a gift. In no way is it a reward for anything *we* have done. What we remember and celebrate this day is the *sole* source of our salvation: we are healed *not* by *our own* good works, and not by *our* faith, but rather by the cross of the incarnate Christ. Thus, our liturgy is itself a warning against the persistent danger of reducing religion to the level of an insurance policy—as if *faith* or *works* were premiums paid in this life for dividends to be collected in the life to come. Such a distortion is simply idolatry. It implies that we are gods who can save ourselves, and who, therefore, have no need for the healing of the Lord's cross.

Then there are those who misuse the cross by using it to symbolize a *hard* life, a life "ordained by God" which, when borne patiently, would produce its reward in the end…at the very end, meaning heaven. This kind of piety excuses hunger, unem-

Chapter 6 • Suffering

ployment, destitution and injustice as "all parts of the cross" to be accepted as "one's lot in life." And so we tell the poor to "offer it up!" We need to cancel that kind of thinking. Of course, there will be suffering. Our imperfect condition will insure that, without violence, greed and misused power adding their enormous burdens to the problem. It is a gross abuse to use the cross as justification for an unjust social order.

Then, there are those who believe self-induced pain is a way to understand the reality of the cross. We forget that the *first* cross came as a consequence of Jesus' preaching and ministry. It was neither willed by God nor deliberately sought by Jesus. Rather the cross was something that happened to him because of human selfishness, and his fidelity to his mission. What he taught and lived set the world of the powerful on its ear. So he was opposed and so he died.

The hymn in Philippians demonstrates how God *in* Jesus comes toward us to be at-one-with-us. "He emptied himself and took the form of a slave—being born in the likeness of humankind." This God-man did not condemn or punish—even when rejected by those he came to heal. "Rather," Paul says, "he humbled himself—obediently accepting death, even death on a cross." The fruit of this twofold self-emptying—first as God, then in his humanity—*is* our salvation. The risen One whom we acknowledge as Lord is truly *our* Lord. From the wood of the manger to the wood of the cross, he is one-with-us. The Father now looks at humanity in the face of his Son.

There is no cheap or easy answer when we struggle to understand the cross. What we don't realize is how much religion costs. C. S. Lewis wrote: "Pain insists on being attended to. God whispers to us in our pleasures, speaks to us in our conscience, but shouts to us in our pain. It is God's megaphone to rouse a deaf world." We tend to think religion is a big electric blanket—a warm fuzzy, when, of course, it inevitably involves the cross. It is much harder to believe than not to believe.

The "Triumph of the Cross" appears to be an oxymoron, a contradiction. But, it says three things about God: First, God does not initiate human suffering. Second, God does not decree it. Third, God bears it with us—weeps with us. Jesus triumphed over his own cross, was raised from the dead, was exalted. Yet Jesus, in one sense, remains in agony *in us* till the end of time for we *are* his body, the Church... *in* the world. We therefore are not *alone* in enduring it; we are not alone. This is the basis of all our hope—the key truth in facing the cross with calm, even peace of mind, and perhaps, with a touch of triumph; we do it together, not alone.

In a few minutes, we will share the bread broken and the wine poured out, that we might be at one with our God. The clearest evidence that we are not alone, that we are reconciled to our God, is our union with one another, the saving gift that we would give to others, "through, with, and in the Lord."

Chapter 7

BEATITUDES

THEN & NOW

Blest are the poor in spirit;　　Blest are the greedy;
　　God's reign is theirs.　　(profit is all they have)

Blest too are the sorrowing;　　Blest are the nervously happy;
　　they shall be consoled.　　(they shall be uncomfortable)

　　Blest are the lowly;　　Blest are the highly;
they shall inherit the land.　　(they shall lose the kingdom)

Blest are they who hunger;　　Blest are they who are full;
　　they shall be filled.　　(they shall be hungry)

　　Blest are the merciful;　　Blest are the indifferent;
　　mercy shall be theirs.　　(nothing shall be theirs)

Blest are the single-hearted;　　Blest are the wishy-washy;
　　for they shall see God.　　(they shall see nothing)

　　Blest are the peacemakers;　　Blest are the warmakers;
they shall be God's children.　　(they shall remain orphans)

Chapter 7 • Beatitudes

GIVE THANKS

Deuteronomy 8:7–18; 1 Timothy 6:6–11,17–19;
Luke 12:15–21

Those are strange words for Thanksgiving Day! Somewhat stern, brooding, moralizing, putting the knife of conscience into the heart and turning it. Why on Thanksgiving? Why not a little more upbeat, a little more gentle? Perhaps the words suggest that all we have to give thanks for amounts to *nothing* unless it is shared, that all things we *are* thankful for become no-thing, nothing, if they are not shared. Whether it is wealth, or power, or time, or talent or whatever—it all *calls* to be shared. If it is not shared it becomes an object, an idol, to be worshipped. And if I, who am *someone*, enters really into the world of nothing, *no*-thing, I become *some*-thing instead of *someone*. I lose my personhood. My identity is found in nothing…if my life is not shared, poured out, broken, given.

All *things* must be seen in relationship that is the measure of sin. Sin is not the law, the Ten Commandments or the Precepts of the Church. Sin has only to do with how we manage our relationships so that all things must be seen in relationship. There is *nothing* that is not in relationship, so that things only find their value *in* relationship. In faith, we are essentially a communal-relational people, even if we don't *look* like it—even if we embrace individualism or if we embrace nationalism or if we believe in capitalism. In faith *all* things, all reality, all humanity and peoples and nations and races and societies *remain in relationship:* whoever I am, whatever I have, *must be shared.* If it remains unshared, there is nothing to be thankful for.

Thanksgiving—though a secular feast in America—can be appropriated, in faith, if *realized* in community and *experienced* through relationships. So *all* life is then interconnected, and we are all called to be *One*—interconnected; and that's what life is about. If life is not about that, it is not life.

So we cannot give thanks for wealth unless it is shared.

We cannot give thanks for talent unless it is used for others.

We cannot give thanks for having clout, unless it liberates those without clout.

We cannot give thanks for our house or home unless we welcome the stranger.

We cannot give thanks for our comfort unless we provide for the comfort of others.

We cannot give thanks for the food on *our* tables unless we see to it that the tables of the poor are full.

We cannot give thanks for the clothes on our back if we fail to recognize the homeless who are cold.

As Paul suggests: "We brought nothing into this world nor have we the power to take anything out." We will not need a U-Haul on the back of our hearse. We give thanks because we have life—eternal life—*now!*—Paul says, "which is life indeed." We give thanks because we have vision; that is what being a Catholic is, as far as I am concerned. What is important about being Catholic is that we have vision. We know what we are about because we have vision to make all realities become *one* whatever or whoever they are. Only then will the Kingdom come, in all its fullness.

BLESSED ARE THOSE

Zephaniah 2:3; 3:12,13; 1 Corinthians 1:26–31; Matthew 5:1–12

Blessed are those who see that being Christian has little to do with success, power, strength or serenity; the reign of God is theirs.

Blessed are those who are self-forgetful enough to act on God's agenda, rather than their own—they shall find their way.

Blessed are those who can live with God's foolishness, can accept weakness as the inescapable condition for experiencing God's love—they shall know God.

Blessed are those who value the love of family and friends—the brother or sister who is always there, the devoted hospice or soup kitchen worker, the clinic nurse—the reign of God is theirs.

Blessed are those who grieve for the lost and struggle to cope and continue—the single parent trying to raise a family alone—the mother or father who keeps an open heart and outreached hands to the wayward son or daughter—for they shall be comforted.

Blessed are those who find their joy in the happiness of others—the devoted parent, the dedicated teacher, the wise and just corporate manager—for they shall inherit the earth.

Blessed are those who manage to see beyond their own interests and needs…to the greater common good and their responsibility to others—for they will be filled.

Blessed are those who treat classmates, co-workers and employees with respect and dignity, who are truly sensitive to the needs and feelings of others, who remember that they have been forgiven by a loving God, and readily extend that forgiveness and compassion to others—for they will receive mercy.

Blessed are those who dedicate their lives to seeking God's justice in all things…and with their talents and gifts put themselves at the service of others, to help *them* discover the joy of God's presence *in their lives*—for they will see God.

Blessed are the peacemakers—those who possess that rare gift for bringing people together when anger and selfishness threaten to drive them apart, who readily take the first step in forgiving and being reconciled with others, who bring healing to those who have been hurt, forgotten or marginalized—for they are the sons and daughters of God.

> BLESSED ARE THOSE WHO…REMEMBER THAT THEY HAVE BEEN FORGIVEN BY A LOVING GOD, AND READILY EXTEND THAT FORGIVENESS TO OTHERS.

Chapter 7 • Beatitudes

Blessed are those who are persecuted and ridiculed in our world today for what is right and just—parents, teachers, dedicated individuals who stand in opposition to false perceptions, destructive stereotypes, and an ever more alienated and cynical society, those who speak for the needs of children, and justice for the poor, compassion for the fallen and lost, and loving support for the abused—for the reign of God is theirs.

The Beatitudes have been on the biblical shelf for 500 years—too long—leaving us with the Ten Commandments, which have led us to a level of mediocrity. What Jesus proposed is this: humanity's hope lies in the voluntary renunciation of those besetting sins that constantly pit one human being against another. These sins are three: holding, climbing and commanding. *Holding* is the desire to horde the goods of creation, to insure one's life by always grabbing more food, more money, more land and possessions, than one needs. (America, one-sixth of the world's population, consumes 40 percent of the world's goods.) *Climbing* is the impulse to control and manipulate others, to dominate. The church has excelled at this at various times in her history. The rich, even when they reach out to help the poor, do it in a patronizing manner.

"*We* know what's best for you." If the poor were asked in the beginning, they probably would have rejected welfare. Over and against this pattern, Jesus invites us to form a community of voluntary renunciation. Christians are people who freely renounce the impulse to horde, to "make it," to control. The

Beatitudes trace out for us the personal and social conditions that must be met if a genuinely new community is to be formed in our world. Go home and read Paul again. Read the passage over and over again, as it is a complete contradiction to conventional wisdom, and sums up well the meaning of the Beatitudes. God chose those who, in the world's measure, count for nothing, to reduce to nothing those who, in the world's measure, think they are something. Both Jesus and Paul point out the same task for us: we must be willing to change, to accept weakness and vulnerability, to embrace the tough reality of the cross. Concretely, this means that we must not only change our attitudes, but change the way we think and the way we live. We are inconsistent when we maintain that the life-style of Jesus was suitable for Jesus but not for us. We are shortsighted when we claim that we shall accept the doctrine of Jesus but not his behavior. Yet Jesus reveals less in his words than in his life-style. Jesus first *lived* the Beatitudes and then *spoke* them. They came out of his very being. And he reveals not only who God is but what we must become: children of God while being *in the world*.

> WE ARE SHORTSIGHTED WHEN WE CLAIM THAT WE SHALL ACCEPT THE DOCTRINE OF JESUS BUT NOT HIS BEHAVIOR.

Chapter 7 • Beatitudes

GOD IS NOT PREDICTABLE

Ezekiel 2:2–5; 2 Corinthians 12:7–10; Mark 6:1–6

To a pioneering spirit who was discouraged by frequent criticism, the Master said, "Listen to the words of the critic. He reveals what your friends hide from you." But he also said, "Do not be weighed down by what your critic says. No statue was ever erected to honor a critic. Statues are for the criticized."

—Anthony de Mello

Dismal would describe Jesus' reception in his home town. His relatives and acquaintances could not figure him out. Here was someone who grew up in Nazareth, who went to their schools and synagogues and earned his living as a carpenter. Now, all of a sudden, he turns into a wonder worker and starts telling parables that nobody can understand. On one occasion his relatives came to rescue him from his preaching ministry because they thought he was going mad. "They found him too much for them."

Ministry is a losing game. Paul details the long list of his difficulties, including "a thorn in the flesh," that were interfering with his peace of mind. Paul traveled all over the known world proclaiming God's Kingdom, and what does he get? Shipwreck, rejection, imprisonment, stoning, persecution and betrayal. Why could not God, infinitely powerful, do something to smooth the way for the proclamation?

Our God is *not* predictable. This is the point of the parables. They try to prepare our minds for a different set of expectations from the ones we bring with us from childhood, or whatever. Paul was thinking, "I'm working for you, Lord, risking my life for you, and this 'thorn in the flesh' is getting me down." Perhaps Paul had arthritis. Maybe he had an emotional problem. Maybe he was impetuous and had a sharp tongue. Whatever it was, it was serious. He besought the Lord again and again saying, "Let me out of this mess. Help! Help!" And the reply came, "Nothing doing. I prefer the way things are. *My power* is made perfect in *weakness*." This is news. (Would hardly sell on Wall Street.) God is more pleased with our weakness than with our success. Why? Perhaps because for most people success is self-defeating. Until we have been rejected, opposed, and have endured all kinds of difficulties, success is hard to handle. Paul was given big revelations—he could have had big temptations. The experience of our weakness is God's special gift to us. After the divine rejection of his prayer for deliverance, Paul was able to say, "I am going to boast from now on about my *weakness* so that the *power* of Christ may be manifest in me." And it was.

The world of divine assistance is hidden, but real and much more substantial, affirming and liberating than events or situations that *we* are inclined to interpret as God's special blessing or help. The Kingdom of God is active in disappointments, rejection, and opposition of the kind that Jesus experienced from his own household. The Kingdom of God is in the ordinary ups and downs of life; in the daily routines that bring back the same old weaknesses joined to our inability to overcome them. The presence of the Kingdom is manifested in our efforts to keep going, to keep loving, to keep hoping without any evidence that God is helping us. It is life on the edge, life in confrontation with difficulties of every kind. According to Jesus, God identifies with our dilemmas, confusion, struggles, failures. God is present in the sad reflection that after a life-time in God's service, there is seemingly nothing to show for it. Jesus experienced exactly this kind of situation. He just kept going and continued to be "too much for them," wherever he went.

What we are doing in life is not as important as our *attitude* toward what we are doing. That is what God is most interested in. Perhaps that's why we have that word "Beatitude." Let your attitudes be "poor in spirit." The attitude of faith does not limit God's activities to what we see or feel, but recognizes the divine messages that come coded in the events of daily life. A good prayer life enables us to decode the messages within a confused and troubled world. This attitude of faith enables us to say (without presumption), "I'm not going to fight this problem anymore but make the best of the situation. My weakness itself may be a necessary remedy that God has sent me, that I might come to know the full extent of God's mercy." If we are going to connect fully with the mystery of God's love in daily life, our trust in God

> WHAT WE ARE DOING IN LIFE IS NOT AS IMPORTANT AS OUR ATTITUDE TOWARD WHAT WE ARE DOING.

needs to be unlimited. Once we have let go of our preconceived ideas and prepackaged value systems that expect God to fit into the narrow confines of our human judgment, nothing can separate us from the love of Christ. He keeps breaking out of them and inviting us to come along with him…and to be "too much" for the world we live in.

"Gladly," says Paul, "will I boast of my *weakness* that the *power* of God may be fully manifest in me." The power of God becomes greater in the degree that we move beyond our limited ideas of God's action and allow the Kingdom to unfold within us.

AT THIS TIME

"…not as the word of man, but as the word of God at work within you who believe."
—1 Thessalonians 2:7–9,13

Though I walk
through the world
of the human word:
conventional wisdom,

I strive to believe,
   not solely to succeed;
to share, not merely to own;
to free-up, not to control;
to forgive, not to reject,

While listening prayerfully
to the word of God
at work within me.

Chapter 7 • Beatitudes

BEATITUDES OF THE WORLD

Zephaniah 2:3; 3:12,13; 1 Corinthians 1:26–31; Matthew 5:1–12

The disconsolate stockbroker lost a fortune and came to the monastery in search of inner peace, but was too distraught to meditate. After he had gone, the Abbot had a single sentence by way of wry comment. "Blessed are they who sleep on the floor—they never fall from their beds."

—A<small>NTHONY DE</small> M<small>ELLO</small>

To understand the blessings of Jesus we must first contrast them with the blessings proclaimed by the kingdom of this world. It is a very real kingdom with its own demand of allegiance. It holds out promises of blessing to those who serve within it.

What are the beatitudes of the world? They are hard to miss for it is a noisy kingdom. The slogans and seductions that assault us are the easiest to identify. (Super Sunday, TV advertising at $700,000 for 30 seconds.) But commercials are like court jesters of more sinister, cynical rulers. They promise us happiness through which we buy, possess, look like and use. If we go there we will be happier. If we have that, life will be finer. If we use this, we will be better loved. If we dress like so, we will be admired.

The world proclaims its message incessantly and provocatively; it spins its web of deceit with cunning. With flim-flam persuasion, it tells us that the purpose of power is domination...that the purpose of wealth is exploitation…that the purpose of love is manipulation.

The lie of this world says that it is acceptable to abort unborn babies so long as they are called fetuses and so long as our lives are not complicated; that it is whimsical to exploit the poor and corrupt the young and pollute the world so long as we remain comfortable and don't have to see it; that it is fine to kill people in war so long as they have a different color of skin than our own or speak a strange language; that it is okay to electrocute criminals who are mostly poor and black and then provide pleasant prisons for the white-collar crimes; that it is somewhat humorous to "look out for number one" and to walk over others in the pursuit of power. The reason these lies are so persuasive is that they are spoken in camouflaged language—covered by high-sounding and sentiment-arousing words like "freedom of choice" and "patriotism" and "national security." The gospel of the world is a lie—it remains *bad news* no matter how cleverly told. A Mr. Kravis—a self-made billionaire whose wealth has come from leveraged buy-outs—spoke recently to the Tulsa Chamber of Commerce. His message? "Ethics in Business." That was like inviting Rambo to talk on non-violence.

And before we situate ourselves too comfortably within God's Kingdom, let us be aware that when we speak of "the world" we are *not* talking about something that exists completely outside ourselves. We have allowed ourselves to accept some measure of evil as our own measure…assimilated the standards of the world as our own standards.

The words of Jesus, the Beatitudes, are difficult words for us—difficult to understand and difficult to accept. How blessed do we really regard it to be poor? To be persecuted? To be sorrowing? Is this really our understanding of happiness—the definition that drives our days and comforts our nights? Not really. Yet there they are—the Beatitudes, continually calling us to step outside *our* preconceptions of reality and to accept a whole new way of looking at things. If we can accept the premise that somehow happiness can solve sorrow, we can also accept the injunction that we must love our enemies and take up our cross of service to follow Jesus.

> THE GOSPEL OF THE WORLD IS A LIE—IT REMAINS *BAD NEWS* NO MATTER HOW CLEVERLY TOLD.

To be "poor in spirit" involves a variety of characteristics but the most essential is the profound awareness of who we are as creatures before God. This is our sense of dependency. We exist, moment by moment, only because of the creative love and fidelity of the Father/Mother: God. We are naked and powerless before the mystery of our own destiny; when we think about it, it seems obvious. But look how much of our lives is built around the avoidance of just this realization. We construct around ourselves a veneer protection against the simplest fact of all, about us: that we don't belong to ourselves but depend upon another —*the* Other. At times of great stress the smooth veneer of our comfortable non-reflective lives cracks and opens, and we are faced with the abyss of our own nothingness. But we quickly recover and seek distraction: pleasure, possessions, power—anything to keep us from facing the fact that we are not forever in this world.

Poverty of spirit does not seek to sedate the pain of existence with the narcotics of distraction and compulsion, but simply reposes in its own poverty. Because of this, the Beatitudes are marked by a wonderful openness, receptivity and flexibility.

It is precisely *what* we possess, cling to, grasp and clutch at that will keep us from opening to others in trust. When we cease to cling even to our own lives, when we let go of even that most intimate of possessions—our self-estimation—then we are truly open to the entrance of God into our lives. It is a "welcoming" of the God who has held us in being by loving us all along.

God is not a "thing" like other things. When we turn to God, when we do not cling to any "thing" as ultimate; we can see, like St. Francis, all other things as they are—as creatures—and rejoice in them. The poor person is able to leave the land of father and mother and journey to a far place on a promise; the poor person is able to let another go in freedom; the poor person can hand over the body to be broken and poured out for another. The poor person is of the Kingdom. Why? Because the Kingdom consists of those who hear the Word of God and keep it. Only the poor can truly hear it.

UNCLE WALTER

*L*et me share with you a story—a deeply moving and intimate experience I had in June of 1978.

Background: I had an Uncle Walter—one of 14 on my mother's side. According to my mother, Uncle Walter had been a priest—studied in Rome—died in Pittsburgh, Pennsylvania, back in the '20s of a fever of some kind. Some 40 years ago, after my father's death, going through some papers, I discovered that all had not been well for Uncle Walter.

In June 1978 while in Pittsburgh visiting relatives, I probed two of my elder cousins about the mystery of Uncle Walter and then, a few days later, I visited my Uncle Frank in New York City to further unravel the puzzle. My cousins related that Walter, as priest, was a talented man—played the violin, wrote plays, left the priesthood, died in New York City. Between the lines, their message read that Walter was called into the priesthood—not by God, but for Irish ethnic reasons.

My Uncle Frank in New York City was something else! Eighty-eight years old at the time—a practicing architect and a practicing heretic for 60 years—left the church from *intellectual* conviction. I discovered from him (having already learned that Walter went to him when the going got bad) that Uncle Walter, priest, was finally sent to an ecclesiastical penal institution in Montreal to be straightened out. He called Frank (the only one in the Irish clan who accepted him). He called for help…deliverance. Exit Walter to New York City, where he sold subscriptions for a Brooklyn newspaper. Later, through Frank, Walter got a job as bookkeeper in a small Brooklyn hotel, married the housekeeper, had a few happy years and died of tuberculosis.

The experience, of course, reinforced my Uncle Frank's attitude and denouncement of the church as institution. He asked me at lunch, "How could I relate to a system that did *that* to people?"

As my uncle and I talked and I accepted him and respected him—welcomed him—we both became more and more human. I could literally see the invisible load being lifted from him—his 88-year-old eyes brightened and his fragile body relaxed with a 60-year-old sigh of relief. We became, in that instant, not just uncle and nephew but intimate friends.

> IN OUR AMERICAN WAY WE CANNOT SEEM TO ACCEPT WEAKNESS, FAILURE, MORAL MISJUDGMENTS.

In our American way we cannot seem to accept weakness, failure, moral misjudgments. Everything is to be neat and positive and institutionalized—no negative experiences in family life are to be recognized or discussed. Uncle Joe may have a drinking problem but it's best to leave it buried and simply ignore him. Tell the children that Joe just has problems and leave it at that.

Father Henry Nouwen, in his marvelous little book *Reaching Out*, points out—as Jesus did—that only poverty of spirit makes a good welcomer...poverty of *heart* and poverty of *mind*. Anyone who is *filled* only with his or her ideas, concepts, opinions and convictions cannot be a good welcomer. There is no inner space to listen, no openness to discover the gift of the other person. The more mature we become, the more we will be able to give up our inclination to grasp, catch and comprehend the fullness of life...and the more we will be ready to let life *enter* into us.

A good welcomer has to be poor in heart. When our heart is filled with prejudices, worries, jealousies, there is little room for a stranger. In a fearful environment, which is the environment for many families, it is not easy to keep our hearts open to the wide range of human experience—success and failure—connectedness to life as it really is. We must forget ourselves in order to let the other person approach us. We must be able to open up to him and let *his* distinctive personality unfold, even though it may, at times, frighten and repel us. We often keep the other person down and only see what we want to see (as the Irish kept my Uncle Walter down)—then we never really meet the mysterious secret of the other's being. We meet only ourselves. (We only saw my Uncle Walter as priest, never as Walter the person.)

If we do not risk the poverty of openness, our lives will never be graced with the warm fullness of human existence. "He who seeks only himself brings himself to ruin; whereas he who brings himself to nought, for me, discovers who he is." All this is very hard to accept in our contemporary world, which tells us about the importance of power and influence.

Yet the paradox remains: Once we have given up our desire to be fully fulfilled, we can offer our emptiness to others. Once we have become poor in heart and mind, we can be good welcomers.

Poverty of spirit is the *inner* disposition that allows us to take away our defenses. For when we are able to say to another: "Please enter! My house is your house, my joy is your joy, my sadness is your sadness…," then we will have nothing to defend since we have nothing to lose—but *all* to give.

My Uncle Frank died within a year of our meeting—died unreconciled to the church. But that really didn't make any difference, for when he died, he died in the Lord. He will not want for his reward.

Chapter 8

WITNESSING

EVANGELIZATION

We are always invited
to evangelize:
proclaim the Good News
to the unchurched;
assuming evidently
that the evangelizers
to the unchurched
are evangelized, churched.
What does it mean
to be churched?
Does it mean
"going to church,"
"attending Mass,"
"getting grace"?
Or, does it mean
what Jesus said it meant:
those "who hear my word
and act on it."
Do the evangelizers,
the Good Newsers
need to be evangelized
before they evangelize?
Do Catholic Christians
believe the Good News
to be good news?
How do you evangelize
the unevangelized
if the evangelizers
are unevangelized?
Won't the unchurched,

leading the unchurched,
fall into the same pit?
How presumptuous
are Catholic Christians
to believe
that they are churched:
"hear the Word
and act on it"?
And who is to say that the unchurched
are unchurched?
Didn't St. Augustine say somewhere
that there are many
in the kingdom
who are not in the church;
and there are many in the church
who are not in the kingdom?
So perhaps
many of the unchurched
are really churched;
and many of the churched
are really unchurched.
Maybe if those communities
of Catholic Christians,
even imperfectly,
put together in their lives
the kingdom/church or the church/kingdom:
"hear the Word
and act on it,"
the truly unchurched
would be churched, that is,
evangelized:
Good Newsed:
evangel/word
ized/acted on.

TAKING ROOT

Isaiah 49:3,5,6; 1 Corinthians 1:1–3; John 1:29–34

There is an exercise widely used at workshops designed for the training of group leaders, which has been adapted for persons who work with the aged. It goes like this: the leader asks each participant to think of three things about themselves that most clearly define who they are. Choices may include their work or career, or their role as spouse, parent or friend. They are then instructed to discard two of their choices in favor of the one they rank the highest. Lastly, they are told to discard even that item. At this point the leader says: "Now you are ready to identify with the very old." I think of my mother who lived to be 92 years old. She would say to me, "Bill, no one calls me anymore." I would tell her, "Mother, you have outlived all of your friends." Many retirees are not happy with retirement—they have lost their purpose in life.

From the time we are first able to think of ourselves as distinct from other persons we do define *who* we are and usually by role or function. We all know persons whose primary role has been taken from them and who, deprived of that sort of self-worth, cannot adapt to a satisfying or happy life.

Today's readings are about roles—the way certain individuals see themselves and others. John the Baptist is very clear about who he is. "*After* me," he announces, "comes a man who ranks *ahead* of me because he was *before* me." We know precisely what it means and marvel at the succinct way he says it. John waits on another. That is who he is. The role of *servant* is the one he has opted for—freely chosen. In this role is his dignity, his wholeness and his glory. But the power of the story—the striking irony that makes it unique and somehow hard to relate to persons and situations we know—is that the man whom John serves with consuming devotion sees himself in the servant role as well.

The words of the servant in the first reading can span centuries to reflect God's plan for His son: "It is too little for you to be my servant...to restore the survivors of Israel. I will make you a light to the nations that my salvation may reach to the ends of the earth."

The church then, being the Body of Christ, must see herself in the servant role as well, and through that service being a light to the nations.

Paul's words to the Corinthians still speak to us as each of us is called to gather in union with Christ as his servants and reflect in our own lives his lifestyle. The basic question is: Do we really want to be servants? Are we willing to be the "town pump" that is there for all to use? Do we really want to let Jesus be reincarnated in *our* humanity?

> ARE WE WILLING TO BE THE "TOWN PUMP" THAT IS THERE FOR ALL TO USE?

Jesus is the "person for others." If we *give* ourselves to him, he will immediately put us in the service of others in one way or another. Do we really want to volunteer for this life of loving service? We can't do it on our own; the Spirit of Christ must do it *in us* and *within* community.

We may not be able to take courageous stands as the Jesuits did in El Salvador, but each one of us can proclaim Christ's servanthood—in less dramatic but in no less profound ways: in our unfailing compassion for others, in our uncompromising moral and ethical values, in our everyday sense of joy and purpose. Every year I get a form asking for the *number* of baptisms, confirmations, children in religious education, etc., for compiling statistics of U.S. Catholics. Nowhere on this form are questions asking about the quality of life in the parish, sacramentally or socially, what impact we have on the community-at-large, or our concern for the poor. It is strictly quantity versus quality.

Hopefully, we are a parish and a church that finds meaning and fulfillment in the role of servant. "You are my servant," says the Lord, "through whom I show my glory!" If *this* is the image others have of us—the servant image—as they *watch* us in their midst, as they *read* pronouncements in the newspaper and *see* how we, as church, spend our energy and resources, then today's readings have taken root.

I suspect there is still much gardening to do.

Chapter 8 • Witnessing

I AM THE PRODIGAL SON

*Joshua 5:9–12; 2 Corinthians 5:17–21;
Luke 15:1–3,11–32*

No other parable communicates better the outrageousness of God's love for us. And it further tells us a lot about ourselves, about what it means "to be" and to be a witness of that outrageous love in a world where mercy is missing. So let the parable weave its way into our minds and hearts and allow each character in the story to draw out of us those things in us that correspond to the part played, so that the part serves to reveal true dimensions of ourselves. So ham it up for a moment and enter into the drama with me.

I am the prodigal son (daughter). There is a me (and a you) that wants what's mine and wants it now; a me that wants to be moving, that doesn't want to be tied down, typed, pigeon-holed; a me that recoils from routine and paternal or maternal expectations; a me that wants to hang loose, live without too many boundaries, that wants to be flexible, that finds "here" somewhat stifling and wants to be someplace else (where the grass is greener). There is a me that is restless, that can't sit still; a me that runs and runs and runs and ultimately gets nowhere; a me that suffers let-down, boredom, no matter how far I run, experiencing the latest place or situation as actually more unsatisfying than the last.

Then there is a me (the prodigal son or daughter) coming to his (her) senses, who feels a tinge of guilt

—not much, but enough to move this me; who suddenly becomes humble; who wants the familiar, after all, on any terms; a me who is ready to purchase a limited amount of comfort, security, routine, predictability at any price; a more modest me who concludes now that limited ambition, limited expectations are more likely to pay off with some regularity.

> THERE IS A ME (THE PRODIGAL SON) COMING TO HIS SENSES, WHO…WANTS THE FAMILIAR ON ANY TERMS.

What a complex person! Fluctuating between ambition, independence, freedom, mobility on the one hand, and modesty, nostalgia, subordination, a longing for routine on the other; fluctuating between self-affirmation and guilt. But in either case seeking peace, fulfillment.

And then there's that dimension of myself that finds this fluctuating side aggravating. There is this elder brother, judgmental me, the me that can't stand the inconsistency, the instability of the adolescent me. I sit in judgment on this aspect of myself and say to my inconsistent self, "Your boredom, your disappointments are your fault. If you would only grow up, toe the line, settle down and do what everyone else does, you'd be all right. But no, you think you're somewhat special. You have to be different. You have to pursue novelty, flit about (like a butterfly in heat) from one interest to another, from one experience to another. So you're bored, crestfallen, unfulfilled. Good! Maybe you'll shape up someday and accept your place, do what you're sup-

Chapter 8 • Witnessing

posed to do, fit in (like I do)!" This elder brother side of myself is a bit sour, perhaps even envious of the adolescent me, but well insulated from frustration and disappointment, because I have learned to expect little, and venture little, and risk little.

Now the father (mother) me enters the scene. I am generous, indulging the adolescent me. I let him (her) be. I don't condemn. There is a me that permits, forgives, receives back without judgment; that brushes aside the selfish stupidity of the prodigal me, and, at the same time, is patiently bemused by the pretensions of the dutiful, if priggish, elder son. The father (mother) me picks up the pieces without blaming the me that is propelled by heart and understanding, and not by analysis and standards; a me that is faithful, that pays no attention to the boundaries of propriety; that embraces me as I am, with all my fluctuations, ups and downs; that takes all that and says, "Look, forget it. Let's be, let's live, let's have a party!"

This is the me that understands and tolerates all my curiosity and quests for freedom and fulfillment, and then patiently waits for me to come back to the *now*, to discover the possibilities of celebration contained within the *present* place and moment; a me that is fundamentally, absolutely, magnanimously merciful, that cultivates *being* without constraint—my own and that of others…not cultivating *doing* without constraint, but being; that is, presence, real presence—openness, unconditional acceptance, mercy without limits; a me that is convinced that out of *mercy* surprises come, and profound merriment. This is why we call the gospel *Good News!*

AT THIS TIME

"...even though the disciples had locked the doors..."
—John 20:19–31

I lock my car door
    my garage door
    my house door
    my office door
    for fear of thieves...

...and the door
    to myself
    for fear that Jesus
    might steal in
    and take my heart.

WHO DO YOU SAY THAT I AM?

Matthew 16:13–20

"Do not be afraid, it is I!"
"Lord, if it is really you..."
"Who do they say I am?"
"Who do you say I am?"

These passages are filled with questions originating within our human experience of fear and wonder. For the disciples, who were victims of a violent storm—and did not under-

Chapter 8 • Witnessing

stand Jesus too well—the questions are similar to the ones we ourselves sense deep in our hearts: "Who do *I* say he is?" When we find ourselves stressed by the troubles in our personal or public lives, we may well wonder where Jesus is, whether we can trust that he is indeed to be found in our faith community, in our sacramental life...in the Word proclaimed. And often we have to "walk on water," take risks, do what seems impossible—to find out that indeed Jesus is with us in this worst of times.

Let me share with you precisely what I mean by "walking on water." I am not talking about magic or science and wonders. I have just returned from my visit to a convent in Pittsburgh, Pennsylvania. As most of you know, I have an aunt there who is a nun. She professed her vows 80 years ago last Sunday. She is now 101 years old and very sound in mind, as she ordered me around all the time I was there. It is a wonderful community, my room was air-conditioned and the refrigerator was full of beer. Now, this is an upbeat community, Sisters of St. Joseph of Baden, Pennsylvania. Like most communities, it is an aging community, but they are undertaking something that reminds me of "walking on water." They are getting ready to build an extensive unit on their property that will take care of the elderly poor of the Ohio River Valley in which they live. One-third of the building will be used for their own sisters, two-thirds will be for the elderly poor of the greater community north of Pittsburgh.

Here is a community that professed one woman last Sunday, took on, I think, three novices, a community of 300 or 400 nuns; a community where many are quite old, but a community which is looking at that situation and is still moving ahead to serve the poor, going through extensive expense, costs and dedication, but hopefully believe that Christ is with them and, by golly, they are going to do it. That is what I mean by "walking on water." It was a great experience. The women of the church, especially the nuns, are light years ahead of us. At other, more peaceful times—times of quiet prayer—we are challenged to proclaim, "You are the Christ"—the Way, the Truth, the Life.

(As a humorous situation, I said Mass every morning, preached a little. When I took the pulpit the first morning, there were two versions of the gospel sitting there, the traditional version and then they had the inclusive language version which was a surprise, as we use it here quite often. I shared with them the inclusive version of Scriptures. My experience is with nuns being way out ahead of the church and these ladies are, indeed, walking on water.)

We may have to move beyond secondhand answers—what theologians are saying—or even the answers of our faith community. For our response to Jesus' question "Who do you say I am?" is more than a simple answer to a question, as if we were thumbing through a catechism; it is an acknowledgment of our deepest relationship with

Chapter 8 • Witnessing

Jesus...in the company of believers, a giving of our trust, a word that contains our *whole* lives not just our lives compartmentalized into spiritual or worldly. In effect, it means moving beyond the shallows of doubt and mistrust into the deep waters of faith.

Discipleship is a school in which the examinations are held at times we cannot always anticipate. And the purpose of the exam is not so much to discover whether we know the right answer, as whether we can provide the password into a deeper relationship with the Lord. It may be through the admission that we don't measure up and need this Savior...need his power and presence, not just the world's, or it may be in acknowledging that we have lost our way (and surely we have) and that Jesus alone is the way to the Father. It may come down to the experience of asking of others the question in relationship to ourselves: "Who do you say I am?" How else will I discover who I am?

When you want to strike back at your spouse with a sharp word, or worse—"Who do you say I am?"

When a quick financial killing can be made simply by putting your ethics on hold for a little while—"Who do you say I am?"

When you're about to join in the taunting of one of those "uncool" kids in the school-yard—"Who do you say I am?"

When that obnoxious, self-righteous stupid bore in the office has pushed you to the edge—"Who do you say I am?"

When your son or daughter needs help with that school project and the newspaper remains to be read —"Who do you say I am?"

When yet another appeal is made to your time, or your wallet, on behalf of the sick, the poor or troubled—"Who do you say I am?"

Passing the exam of discipleship takes a lifetime and we gradually, day by day, come to realize more deeply "who *he* is," as we struggle in faith to become who we say *we* are *in him*. That is, as we offer ourselves as a test case of our own proclamation, as a people transformed by the Spirit in a community of faith, love, hope and thoughtfulness…a people who finally and hopefully *know who they are.*

AT THIS TIME

"He makes the deaf hear and the mute speak."
—Mark 7:31–37

Would someone
please bring me,
deafened as I am
by the din of media,
to the Lord's Word?
Would someone
please bring me,
tongue-tied as I am,
tripping over untruths,
to the Lord's wisdom?

TRANSMIT AND RECEIVE

Isaiah 53:10,11; Hebrews 4:14–16; Mark 10:35–45

The Master was known to favor service over withdrawal. But he always insisted on 'Enlightened' service. The disciples wanted to know what 'Enlightened' meant. Did it mean 'right-intentioned?' "Oh no," said the Master. "Think how right-intentioned the monkey is when he lifts a fish from the river to save it from the watery grave."

—Anthony de Mello

James and John wanted to share the realm of Christ—to sit at his right and left. They may have been right-intentioned, but hardly enlightened, because for them, it meant being superior…arriving at some kind of false fullness.

For many of us, like James and John, wholeness means "getting it together," being on top, being in the know, aware. Wholeness will provide a vantage point from which to judge more clearly than we could when we were ignorant, full of reflexes; it will enable us to make the "right" decisions. It means a smoother existence, power at last after so much surrounding of life to fears and conditioning, to the institutions and individuals that muted so much of our potential to be. Is this what fulfillment or wholeness means to us? To get above it all? To be superior, special, more comfortable, less hassled, more in charge of things after years of being buffeted around—at the mercy of fears, conditioning circumstances of life? It sounds like Christ would find that approach to wholeness disturbing. If we seek wholeness in order to be on top, secure, right, clear, able to detect mistakes, and avoid them, like some fantasy hero of the movies, then we approach wholeness right intentioned, maybe, but not enlightened.

We become whole, when—knowing our hypocrisies, our mistakes, our ignorance, the inaccuracy of our assumptions, the way we deceive ourselves and others, our fears, our tendency to act before we think, our tendency to jump to conclusions—we *embrace* all that with mercy and understanding, drink it down, consume it, *own* it with mercy and understanding.

> HOW CAN CHRIST EMPOWER US UNLESS THROUGH OUR VERY POWERLESSNESS?

We start to become whole, when—knowing how other individuals or institutions have shaped our own lives, filled us with the need to be perfect, to be cautious, to be secure, laid upon us in inflexible rubrics for living and doing—we drink it down with mercy and understanding, consume it, own it, own our relationship with the whole of humanity's fears and betrayals, with mercy and understanding.

We start to become whole, when—knowing the limitations of human existence, the vulnerability of our bodies and minds, the immensity and variety of the universe, the mortality, the passing nature of ourselves and everything around us, the unpredictability of so much…in sum, the irreducible mystery of life—we do not back off but drink it all down, consume it, own it, immerse ourselves in it with a sense of abandon, belonging, trust, *service.*

Isaiah tells us that it was "*because of his affliction*" that the prophet will see the light in the fullness of days. And Paul tells us, "We do not have a high priest who is unable to sympathize with our *weakness,*" and Mark tells us in his story of Jesus, "Whoever wants to rank first among you must *serve* the needs of all." Drinking down, consuming, owning our own limitations enables us to reach out to others, not from power but out of weakness. For how can *Christ* empower us unless through our very powerlessness? God's love took flesh through Christ's weakness—in his humanity, not through his divinity. Christ's love takes flesh through our humanity—in our weaknesses, not through our strengths. And finally he is saying to us that we do not *choose* to suffer—that would go against nature and good sense. It is *service* that we choose. There will be suffering enough if we choose to serve.

As we live we are *transmitters* of life. And when we fail to transmit life (even in our weakness), life fails to flow through us and we die even though alive. We are also *receivers.* Life is around us to take in, to embrace, to be enjoyed, to rest in, to grow in and be made whole again.

LAUGHTER, MUSIC, AND GOOD RED WINE

Acts 1:15–17,20–26; 1 John 4:11–16; John 17:11–19

The Master was in an expansive mood, so his disciples sought to learn from him the stages he had passed through in his quest for the divine. "God first led me by the hand," he said, "into the Land of Action, and there I dwelt for several years. Then He returned and led me to the Land of Sorrows; there I lived until my heart was purged of every inordinate attachment. That is when I found myself in the Land of Love, whose burning flames consumed whatever was left in me of self. This brought me to the Land of Silence, where the mysteries of life and death were bared before my wondering eyes." "Was that the final stage of your quest?" they asked. "No," the Master said. "One day God said, 'Today I shall take you to the innermost sanctuary of the Temple, to the very heart of God!' And I was led to the Land of Laughter."

—A<small>NTHONY DE</small> M<small>ELLO</small>

Hilaire Belloc, the Catholic English writer and convert, on one of his verses announces: "Wherever the Catholic sun does shine, there is music and laughter and good red wine. At least I've found it so. Benedicamus Domino!" For several Sundays now, Jesus has been talking about his joy being ours, that we might share his joy completely.

Chapter 8 • Witnessing

Those who were "witnesses to the resurrection" were called by Jesus to witness...but to be careful in doing so; to abide in God's love, God's joy, God's laughter. Unfortunately, and to the contrary, we have often been grim, somber and dour, preoccupied with sin, damnation and guilt—solemnly insisting on obedience to the *letter* of multitudinous laws and rules, and so uptight about our faith as to be unable to relax and enjoy ourselves. In the old days, those who decided to become Catholics rarely mentioned that it was the joyfulness of Catholics that attracted them. Do we remember the first time we laughed heartily in church? (No thunderbolts from heaven?)

There is a lot of talk about evangelization today, but some folks seem to confuse evangelization with high-pressure, mass media publicity, or with organizational door-to-door membership drives, or with so-called "convert making" techniques. This is hardly the essence of evangelization. The heart of evangelization is joyous, carefree, happy love while serving others. What else? It cannot be a smothering, sticky, sweet love by those who *oppress* other people by their love, which, in fact, is merely skillful manipulation. It must be the kind of love that leaves others free to make their own choices. We cannot approach others with the pretense of knowing the answers to what life really means if we do not, by the kind of lives *we* live, demonstrate that *our* faith *does* put meaning into our lives, and makes us more generously caring, more humane, more compassionate, and *free* within our own self-esteem and our relationship to others. We cannot short-circuit the process; we cannot substitute sophisticated gimmickry and hard sell for the witness of a responsibly free, mature, generous, loving life. We should *look like* who we *say* we are.

How close do we "Catholic Christians" approach the ideal of joy expressed in "laughter and music and good red wine"? How do we become carefree? Perhaps, more to the point, why should we be carefree? Are there not enough cares and worries in the world to keep us mired indefinitely? Is it not false to be joyous? Should we not be somber and soberly serious because that is precisely the appropriate response to the mess the world is in? Is not the sour-faced saint, in fact, the good Christian? Is not his or her sour face reflecting the absurd state of our society? What is there to be hopeful about?

> EVEN DEATH ULTIMATELY YIELDS TO THE POWER OF GOD'S LOVE. EXTRAORDINARY!

That question, of course, brings us to the essence of Christianity, a religion whose center is *Good News*. Indeed, the *Good News* is that our God's forgiving, reconciling, saving love, is far stronger that all the evil, all the tragedy, all the suffering in the world…and might even move *us* to change, and thereby change the world. Even death ultimately yields to the power of God's love. Extraordinary! Even death dies under that power. It is just that simple. We *believe* it, then necessarily we *live* lives of joy and hopefulness. We will then be truly, fundamentally carefree, for "we have come to know and believe in the love God has for us. God is love and we who abide in love abide in God, and God in us." Hopefully, we find it so. Benedicamus Domino!

A HOLY MOMENT

John 14:1–12

To a preacher
who kept saying,
"We must put God in our lives,"
the Master said,
"God is already there.
Our job is to recognize this."

—Anthony de Mello

Jesus changes forever the notion of *what* is holy and *where* it is to be found. With the Gospel of John comes the insight that the divine is not aloof; rather it is intimate and self-giving. Through Christ's Spirit this self-givingness has come to stay *within* the human. We do not have to move to some kind of divine level to come into contact with the holy: rather it is *through* contact with the *human* that the *sacred* is experienced.

"Our job is to recognize this."

Yet the words of John provoke the community of his time to discern how the love of God continues to pulse through our *human* reality. "Philip, how can you say, 'Show us the Father'? Do you not believe that I am in the Father and the Father is in me?" In the very beginning of John's Gospel, in the great prologue, we read, "The Word became flesh; he came to dwell among us." We have, of course, ever since then made frantic efforts to change the flesh back into words…words, words, words. Words from scholars, words from preachers, words from teachers…words, words, words. We have been through a blizzard of words, belittled the incarnation. "The Word became flesh." The Word did not become word: "The Word became flesh."

"The Word came to *dwell* among us"—to live, to abide, to fully enter the human condition. And since that Final Word of God is risen and lives, then that Word still became flesh, still abides in us and with us, through His Spirit. But, unfortunately, we have reduced the Word to words. We have taken his flesh from him and dry bones remain. Small wonder that the world still asks, "Show us the Father." Small wonder that religion is lifeless and boring. Remember the story of Jesus restoring life to Jairus' daughter? Jesus in the midst of the wailing and moaning, clamor and din, restores the child to life: "Little girl, get up." And she does. And then he says an astonishing thing: "Give her something to eat" (words of flesh). We would have said, "Take her to the church to pray," we who are more spiritual than God.

The incarnation, "the Word becoming flesh," is a scandal—unsophisticated, undignified of God, a bit absurd. And so, we have made the Word sophisticated, dignified, logical, by reducing the Word to dogmas, to propositions, to creeds. Small wonder the world still asks, "Show us the Father." When they ask, we hand them a catechism.

Where do we think that people still meet the Word? Where do we really find and experience the "holy"? Does the Word take flesh—in a church, at a revival, on retreat, or on evangelical television?

Today is Mother's Day. When a mother is concerned about her sick child, she attends to the child's needs. The child is lying there in bed and suddenly wakes up and looks up at mother and smiles, eyes grow bright. *That is a holy moment.* That's what it is all about. It is not about anything else.

Let me share with you my own experience of working at the Neighbor for Neighbor Clinic in North Tulsa, every Thursday afternoon, for 20 years. What I share is also being experienced at the Green Country Free Clinic on the west side of Bartlesville. Now, obviously, we can't all volunteer at clinics or soup kitchens…whatever, but all of us can, in many small ways, be the Word-made-flesh for others in responsible, gentle and loving relationships.

The folks on the west side of Bartlesville or at Neighbor for Neighbor meet the Word-made-flesh when they sit across the desk from the volunteer during in-take. "In-take"—one of those funny clinical words we use—is "taking in" *that* person, at that moment, with unconditional personal regard for the whole person sitting there, flesh and blood and spirit…the interviewer creating a kinder, gentler environment for the sick. *That is a holy moment.* People meet the Word-made-flesh through the nurses' loving touch, the nurse who makes no judgment about the patient's clothes or smell or lice in the scalp. *That is a holy moment.* People meet the Word-made-flesh through the competence, sense of humor, and serious care of those filling prescriptions…words on paper taking flesh in healing medicine. *That is a holy moment.* People meet the Word-made-flesh through the doctors whose skilled hands, intelligent mind and gentle heart listens well and responds with compassion. *That is a holy moment.* People meet the Word-made-flesh through the medical technicians who patiently and carefully test the body fluids. *That is a holy moment.*

The Word doesn't float somewhere in mid-air touching down occasionally to perform signs and wonders. The Word of God needs *flesh* to act, to reach out, to touch, and the *only* flesh the Word has is *ourselves*. Ourselves…not just because we volunteer, not just because we are there, but because of *our* personal, faithful, *real* presence to that particular person…because *we are* the body and blood of Christ in that deeply human moment and meeting. Jesus has changed forever the notion of *what* is holy and *where* it is to be found. And the world out there that is still asking, "Show us the Father," should be able to meet *us*, this community of faith, and profess:

"Yes, we have come to believe
that you are in Christ
and Christ is in you.
Yes, you have shown us the Father."

God is already there—our job is to recognize this.

Chapter 9

SPIRITUALITY

TUNNEL VISION

Tunnel vision
visits anyone
who believes
the world's word
to be wisdom
source of values
attitudes
way of life

yet invariably
our holy Roman nose
peers out
through secular shrouds
smelling an odor
of order
quite other than
the very local
noosepaper
ensnaring us
with its blend
of editorial marshmallows
of bland
tentative truths

or the very worldly
Wall Street Journal
a jaunt through
that ever, ever land

of security through success
of power through prosperity
of influence through
   affluence
lived out within
the established disorder
per omnia
saecula saeculorum
permeated with greed
our nation's present
primal virtue

a vice
which the Real Word
names evil
even if
our very
irreverent reverends
believe and proclaim
electronically
and moronically
the pious piffle
that wealth
is a blessing
upon those
who believe
in America
as God's best

Chapter 9 • Spirituality

and last
word to the world

as if democracy
and free enterprise
are God's final
incarnations
(God forbid!)
but certainly not
fleshed
in Christ Jesus
risen and present
as loser, not winner
as servant, not ruler
as giver, not taker
as sharer, not owner

ultimately
the only Real Word
worth speaking
worth hearing
worth doing
in whom we live
move
have our being
values
attitudes
way of life

all the while
dwelling in
the real world
yet being "other"

(a synonym
for sanctity)
being kingdom-minded
peopled in God
Body of Christ
in whom
with whom
through whom
Christ is in agony
until the end

the end
hopefully
not being
the end
but the world
"passing away"
into the kingdom's
fullness.

Amen.

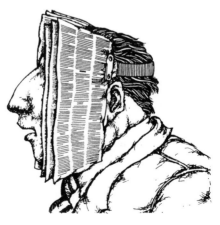

SET THE SPIRIT FREE

In a children's book, *Dragon Kite of the Autumn Moon*, it is the capacity to let go of the heart's most beloved treasure that makes possible the release of healing energy in the world. Set in the midst of Taiwanese traditions surrounding Kite Day, this is the story of a boy, Tad-Tin, and his beloved grandfather. The grandfather, who has always made kites for them to fly together, lies ill—too ill to make a kite to fly in the annual Kite Day celebrations.

In order to participate, Tad-Tin must fly his cherished dragon kite, made by his grandfather years earlier to mark Tad-Tin's birth. Tradition determines that every kite must be set free at the end of the day, so that they will carry all troubles away with them, but Tad-Tin aches at the thought of releasing the magnificent dragon. When he does summon the courage to let the kite soar, he returns home to discover his grandfather miraculously restored to health.

> UNLESS WE LET GO OF OURSELVES, THE SPIRIT WILL NOT COME.

As in the transition from Ascension to Pentecost, this story attests to a central mystery of human faith experience: we must let go of our most beloved treasure in order for it to be returned to us. "If I don't leave you," says Jesus, "the Comforter will not come to you."

I suspect that our most beloved treasure is ourselves. Unless we let ourselves go or let go of ourselves, the Spirit will not come. If the Spirit does not come, we can never truly be ourselves...and if we cannot be ourselves, we will not be the "Good News" to others.

CHRIST KINGSHIP

1 Corinthians 15:20–26,28; Matthew 25:31–46

I am two years older than Mickey Mouse, and the same age as Christ the King. The Feast of Christ the King is not an ancient one. It was founded in 1925, the year I was born. The first church in the world named after Christ the King is the parish in Tulsa, the parish I grew up in; the completion of the building coincided with the founding of the feast.

One of the strange factors that seems to have figured in this feast's beginning was the establishment of the anti-clerical government in Mexico where priests and the religious were being put to death with the words, "Viva Christo Rey" on their lips ("long live Christ the King"). The claims for Christ's Kingship, then, have a connection with the way the Catholic Church has found itself something of an orphan in the modern world. By claiming *Christ's* Kingship, the church was able to proclaim a higher form of sovereignty, a rule that transcended the power of nation states which had done so much harm to the church itself.

Christ's Kingship made demands for allegiance that went beyond citizenship in an individual nation's state. The counterculture, "over and against" character of this proclamation is easily missed here in America, because the Kingship of Christ was easily romanticized, or spiritualized, and had no political content whatsoever. That's why Catholics are still shocked to hear of *Catholic* conscientious objectors who refuse to serve in the armed services on the basis of moral and religious belief. (I mean, after all, they really shouldn't take their faith *that* seriously—should they?)

But the symbol of Christ's Kingship, like the symbol of the reign of God, has to have *some* bite in it when it comes to everyday life. It has to have *some* "political" meaning, or else bringing the liturgical year to an end without it makes our liturgy nothing but a quaint idea, a faith without flesh, a denial of the Incarnation.

What kind of politics does the feast speak about? The gospel is pretty blunt about that. Here the "king" is none other than the Son of Man—the human one, who because of his humiliation and death on the cross, has a special bond with the poor, the outcasts, the homeless. It is not a sentimental bond that says he "feels" for them. Jesus identified not only with all humanity, but most especially with forgotten, oppressed, victimized and desperate human beings. The image of Jesus as the "man on the street" or the "woman in trouble" is a scandalous one, as it was to the

Chapter 9 • Spirituality

pious and selfish in the parable itself. They question him: "When did we see *you* hungry, thirsty, in prison?"

Christ's Kingship does not give the church power *over* kings and emperors, presidents and congressmen, but rather incarnates—gives flesh to—Christ's radical oneness with our broken human condition. The king is really "every person" going about the country rescuing the poor, redeeming the debtor, feeding the hungry.

But to those of us on his left, the Son of Man will say, "Out of my sight!" For when a group home for the mentally handicapped was opened in our neighborhood, we said, "Not in my backyard." When efforts were made to establish low-cost housing for the poor, we took legal action in order to protect real estate values. When workers were subjected to unhealthy working conditions and slave wages, we preached the old bromides of "marketplace forces" and "supply and demand." When a soup kitchen opened in our town, we demanded the police drive away those crazy, dangerous vagrants. When efforts were made to reform health care and guarantee health coverage for *all* Americans, we demanded to know why *we* should pay more for someone else's problems.

And then, *both* the sheep and the goats recognized the face of the Son of Man. He was the mentally handicapped neighbor, the homeless mother of

> THE SON OF MAN…HAS A SPECIAL BOND WITH THE POOR, THE OUTCASTS, THE HOMELESS.

two small children, the poor laborer, the dirty vagrant, the unemployed husband desperate to find medical care for his dying wife.

Christ will hand over the Kingdom to his Father when *we work* with Christ's Spirit to *realize* that Kingdom *on earth* as it is in heaven—*on earth* as it is in heaven.

AT THIS TIME

"…*the time is fulfilled*…"
—Mark 1:12–15

It is time
   (Mark says
   "immediately")

to let the spirit
   drive me, thrust me
   into the wilderness of
   silence and self-dying

away from the wild beasts,
   the glitz of grabbing,
   of owning, having,
   getting

in order to be quiet,
   shut up, let go, give in
   to the Good News;
   come into God's dominion
   and find fulfillment.

Chapter 9 • Spirituality

MUTUAL RELATIONSHIPS
Isaiah 5:1–7; Philippians 4:6–9; Matthew 21:33–43

It intrigued the congregation to see their rabbi disappear each week on the eve of the Sabbath. They suspected he was secretly meeting with the Almighty, so they deputed one of their number to follow him.

This is what the man saw: the rabbi disguised himself in peasant clothes and served a paralyzed Gentile woman in her cottage, cleaning out the room and preparing a Sabbath meal for her.

When the spy got back, the congregation asked, "Where did the rabbi go? Did he ascend to heaven?" "No," the man replied, "he went even higher."

—Anthony de Mello

Mutuality—life given and received in equal amounts—is characteristic of relationships. The reading from Isaiah tells the story of a vineyard that has been well taken care of by its owner but yields sour grapes. Matthew's parable tells a story of a vineyard whose owner also becomes angry but this time at the caretakers rather than the fruit. *Mutuality* is characteristic of relationships. Though the vines were carefully nurtured, they did not produce as expected. The interactional quality was missing.

All life is rational; therefore any notion that we really have control over what will happen is only an illusion. Even in hierarchical structures, power can only be exercised if there is agreement or cooperation; nor can the outcome be forced even when the best circumstances prevail. This can be seen in parent-child relationships. Quite often, parents who provide love and excellent care are stunned when the children don't turn out as they expected. If the parents feel that they should have had complete control over the situation, then they might react with anger and seek to punish.

> WE ARE TO PLACE OURSELVES IN GOD'S HANDS BY PRAYING FOR WHAT WE NEED.

The owner in the second story expects, rightfully, cooperation between himself and his tenants. He sends servants to collect the fruit, but here too there is a refusal of exchange. The tenants take but do not give back. They have come to expect that what has been entrusted to them should be theirs to keep and control. They also want to destroy the goodness of the owner because his presence forces them to see that their way of looking at reality is distorted and false. Not only do they want to own the vineyard, they want no one else to benefit from it. Envy, unlike jealousy, wants first what the other has, but also wants to destroy the other. The tenants, of course, end up destroying themselves.

When we refuse *exchange* in love—refuse to acknowledge the *giftedness* of our lives, and try to possess instead of letting go and sharing—we kill our ability to grow as persons and to love more fully. It is not enough that we are given all the conditions for a full life, we must *accept with gratitude* our *dependence* on God's goodness. Mutuality and *inter*dependence must be present. It is *then*, Paul says, that "God's own peace, which is beyond all understanding, will stand guard over our hearts and minds in Christ Jesus." Paul helps us in our understanding of *how* to respond to life and our humanity by pointing out that we are to feel no anxiety about anything; in everything we must pray and present our *needs*, giving thanks as we do so. In other words, we are to place ourselves in *God's* hands by praying for what we need, rather than trying to control the outcome.

This kind of trust grows out of a relational commitment of giving and receiving rather than controlling and possessing. If we control and possess, we cannot have much of a prayer life. To do this is to acknowledge, for instance, the right relationship between ourselves and creation, between God and ourselves. Nothing is ours because we have earned or deserved it; rather we are the caretakers of our planet, caring for the earth rather than plundering it. We are pilgrims in our relationship with each other and with God. To ask genuinely for our present need in prayer is to experience peace because we are living in the truth of our *dependent* nature. To participate in the exchange of love offered us, we must surrender and be out of control. We exist because God loves us.

Like the rabbi, God came disguised in Jesus, supporting and nourishing us, and we, like the Gentile woman, need to rest in that presence.

THE LAW OF JESUS
Sirach 15:15–20; 1 Corinthians 2:6–10; Matthew 5:17–37

You may be wondering why I have a bandage on my right hand. It is the result of carpal tunnel surgery. It is one of those decisions one has to make. It was a choice: either suffer with the trouble of the hand or have it done away with. I want to thank many of you for your kindness during this troublesome time. It is very interesting how you need two hands, and living alone, it's more interesting. Did you ever try to change a pillowcase with one hand? And, the problem with socks is even worse.

Life appears to be, at times, nothing but one decision after another, and often, these are difficult decisions, like the young person today choosing a career or a school when the economic situation is so volatile. We may live with some fear or anxiety, or experience a deep sense of frustration and even anger, that the need to choose has come our way. At moments like this, it is difficult for us to remember that our free will—our very capacity to reflect, consider or decide—is the essence of our humanness. So the question for Christian people is how are we to navigate our way through the many choices that confront us? Is it simply by adhering to the law? That was the way we were raised up Catholic. Simply follow the law. Matthew keeps in his story the Jewish understanding of the law…as being God's gift to us.

Rather than serving as an arbitrary *limitation* on human freedom, the law's function is to enable us to

Chapter 9 • Spirituality

live more fully. It is one of the paradoxes of the law. Jesus is the fulfillment of the law; in his life and relationships, he embodies the full living-out of the will of God. There is an important distinction to be made here between law as burden—something alien that is imposed from without, what happened to the church growing up—and the law that leads to fulfillment: loving God, serving neighbor, loving self. This is the law of Jesus that leads us to freedom and fulfillment.

We are told that we must be *one* with the law and that we must embody it—live it from the inside out. The center of attention shifts from the extended world where anger and greed are the forces—that leads away from life, toward death. The Wisdom reading zooms in on the basic juncture: the choice between life and death. "Before you," Sirach says, "are life and death." How do we become habituated in this troubled world to making life-giving choices, over choices that I think reflect death? Paul gives us a clue. He says in the reading this morning that the wisdom which "no eye has seen, nor ear heard" is given to those who love God. We began to see a pattern: the love of God draws us to choices that are *for* and *of* life, and as we mature in our ability to make choices *for* life—to live in God's wisdom and not the world's wisdom—we return our love to God. That is what we strive for,

> WE FREQUENTLY MISS THE MARK, AND WE OFTEN UNWITTINGLY CHOOSE DEATH OVER LIFE.

and yet, as our personal and cultural experience gives witness, we frequently miss the mark, and we often unwittingly choose death over life.

Can we really be for life and still be for abortion? Can we really be for capital punishment, 60 million handguns in the U.S., or war, or ignore poverty? Addictions, idolatry and social injustice—all cloud and impede our ability to choose life over death. I was told a true story last week about a courtroom scene involving a divorce action. The husband's lawyer was questioning the wife about an abortion she had. "Did you have an abortion?" he asked. "Yes, I did have," she replied. "Did you have a second abortion?" "Yes," she said. "Could we believe that you had a third abortion?" "Yes," she said. "Shall we try for four abortions?" "No," she replied, "just three." And what was the evidence that she had four abortions? Her MasterCard charge receipts. Interesting world we are living in today. Some would say that she was choosing life. Others would say that she was choosing death. Corporations that decide to "downsize" or "re-structure" (euphemisms for firing people) are choosing death, not life. Yet, in corporate wisdom, they are choosing life—called profits—in the face of death. Troubled times, difficult decisions.

Is the life we are called to merely "spiritual"? Was Jesus' death merely spiritual? Hardly. We are confronted, in faith, with learning to discern in the world, not in church, the difference between paths that end in death and those that pass *through* death to life. The love of God, our openness to God, draws us to choices that are *for* and *of* life, and as we mature in our ability to make choices *for* life to live in God's wisdom and not the world's, we return our love to God.

"Before us," the Wisdom writer says, "are life and death." Always the paradox: my *living* for myself alone is to *choose death*. My *dying* to myself for the sake of others is to *choose life*. A choice of life, however small or imperceptible, is felt in the human heart and reverberates throughout the Kingdom.

AT THIS TIME

"The spirit of the Lord God is upon me..."
—Isaiah 61:1,2,10,11

Is the "spirit
   of the Lord"
   upon *me*...
or is it the spirit
   of individualism,
   racism,
   and greed?

Have I brought
   "glad tidings
   to the lowly..."
or is it more bad news
   for the poor of whom
   I cry "freeloaders!"?

Do I "proclaim liberty
    to captives…"
or do I leave
    the homeless
    and mentally ill
    in the prisons
    of my rejection?

Do I "rejoice heartily
    in the Lord…"
    because I am clothed
    with justice…
or, wrapped in security
    and power,
    do I dwell in gloom?

Chapter 10

COMPASSION

HOSPITAL VISIT

Moving down
from twelve
in the elevator car
the other inmate
glanced at me:
"must have been
a hard case"
she remarked
my body language
speaking
the visit
to Kavanaugh
Chicago roots
nineteen-o-three
railroader
pensioned to
a nursing home

no family here
television
his only visitor
aside from me
stroke left side
amputee right side
massive bed sore
backside
"yes, it was"
as we hit
number one
looking back
she replied:
"let someone
love *you*
tonight"

Chapter 10 • Compassion

CELEBRATING THE ORDINARY

Luke 2:10,11,14

At 9 o'clock this morning I was called to a motel on the west side of town to respond to a couple who had no money, no transportation, and were to be evicted at 11 o'clock. I had helped the woman before—a troubled lady, bouncing from one bad relationship to another, a person dreadfully used. On the phone, I swore softly under my breath, saying to myself: "Where does she get off calling *me* on Christmas morning, a busy priest?" I went out, gave them $40, and wished them a Merry Christmas. Were they conning me? Probably. Should I have gone out? Probably not. But then I said to myself—even the so-called undeserving poor deserve a break on Christmas morning. And the irony of it all? The motel is called the Bartlesville *Inn*. I tell that story because that's what this gospel is all about.

This is the feast where we celebrate the commonplace, the ordinary stuff, blessed and transformed, by the flesh-taking of God…the Incarnation. That word is one of those poetic words. The Word became flesh —our God took flesh. Straw and manger bed became a throne, ox and ass the gracious hosts, and humble, fumbling humanity, the honored visionaries who came to look, and hopefully, what is more, to see and understand. The old tensions between the sacred and earthly dissolve, merge, and grant us peace. It is our own prejudice, not God's, that contrasts the earthly and the heavenly, and finds it ordinary, trite and unimaginative. The divine contradiction is that we find God where we *least* expect Him, within our human condition: in our peak experiences and our sorrows, our successes and especially our failures, our "in loveness" but especially our struggling human relationships—this is the manger bed, these are the places where we will know God, the Word in human vesture.

The whole Christmas story is a fitting sequel to Mary's Magnificat, and a prelude to the beatitudes. This feast teaches us quite simply that in weakness there is strength; it is in our powerlessness that we have power; it is in our emptiness that we become full—that only the humble are exalted. All of which is a total contradiction to the conventional wisdom of our society. Doesn't fit at all. The Church fits too well. We need to be reminded of that on Christmas morning. It follows, then, that in Luke, the first people to hear the gospel would be the shepherds. This fact does not shock us, accustomed as we are to sanitized, Hallmark shepherd boys, carrying immaculately coifed lambs to the manger. In the culture of first-century Palestine, shepherds were marginal characters. Their occupation in relationship to animals made them ritually unclean and so they were perpetual religious outcasts, and I suspect they didn't have too many "precious moments." So these characters with a dubious religious pedigree turn out to be the first audience of the first-century carol.

Luke strikes here a constant note of his Gospel: the God of Jesus had the disturbing tendency to appear among the marginalized and the eccentric. The Good News is this, that it is precisely those places within ourselves that we most fear to look, the parts of ourselves that are most marginal, borderline and eccentric, this is where God is waiting to meet us, not in our security or power or prestige.

The Christmas gospel also invites us deep into ourselves (into the cracks and crannies of our human stuff that we live in) to ponder and to treasure as Mary did. In our weakness, in our powerlessness, we are strong. The Christmas gospel equally compels our gaze beyond ourselves. We can scan the news on television and see the faces of the poor in our cities this Christmas, look closely among the victims of the war in Yugoslavia, or the tragedy in Somalia, or better still, today, glance across the Christmas dinner table at our least favorite in-law. The gaze of the divine child will meet ours and hopefully disarm us.

THE GOODNESS OF GOD

James 1:17,18,21b,22,27

*I*t was a lousy day. It was another rotten, two-bit job. It was the third two-bit job he'd had in four months. And as he wheeled the aged dump truck through the busy intersection, something caught his eye. He pulled the truck over quickly and stopped, for there in the middle of all that traffic were two tiny, gray kittens. He scooped them up, tucked one in each shirt pocket, and drove away. What stops a bitter young man and several tons of truck in the middle of a city street? A kitten you could hold in one hand.

Roses and raindrops, snowflakes and sunsets and kittens: "Every worthwhile gift, every genuine benefit comes from above," says James. Everything good comes into being through the unfailing love and goodness of the God who made the universe with its stars and our little earth…with its sun and moon, and so, everything beautiful, everything good and worthwhile leads, whether we know it or not, back to God.

> EVERYTHING GOOD COMES INTO BEING THROUGH THE UNFAILING LOVE AND GOODNESS OF GOD.

And beauty and goodness and innocence have real power: power to bring an angry young man and his truck to a halt, power to interrupt our routine, to turn us away from ourselves, to slow us down and open our eyes and hearts, to fill us with joy. We've all seen this power in action. We've all seen how a tiny newborn baby will bring out the tenderness of some ordinary, tough, macho male. We've seen how a rambunctious child will suddenly be absorbed in the beauty of a flower, or we've seen how the people of a neighborhood will band together and fight to save a beautiful park. We've all seen the power of beauty and goodness and innocence. But did we ever realize that that power is a

Chapter 10 • Compassion

power that comes from God even when the people involved don't even think of God...from God, the source of every worthwhile gift, every real benefit? And to lose the ability to be touched by this power is to lose what it is to be a human being. To become so callous, so preoccupied with self, so bitter that we no longer feel the sense of wonder at the beauty of the world, any sense of tenderness toward the weak and helpless, any sense of just what the gift of life itself really is, is to become something less than human, something less than what people were made to be.

James saw people like that. He called people with that attitude "the world." And that's why he says: "Keep yourself unspotted by the world." To be *"worldly"* is to see the world as its own beginning, its own end. To be *"worldly"* is to forget that the world is all gift, all grace, all given by a Father/Mother God, who made us to belong to the Creator.

When kittens or snowflakes or the sunset stops us in our tracks—it's a gift! Pure gift! It's when we realize what a gift our world and our lives are that we are really, truly human, when we know that Someone created it in love and keeps it going and we're glad. To see all the world as a gift is important to the way we treat other people, too. If we have any doubt about whether human beings are really worth all the trouble and heartache and pain that it takes to really love and care for them, Christ is our answer. And *pure* worship is to receive everything good and worthwhile as God's gift-in-Christ, and to care for "widows and orphans in their distress." The unfortunate, the grief-stricken, the weak and the sick, the elderly and those without resources—to care for them, to value them as people, as gifts of God, *that is pure worship*. It is pure worship because it springs from a heart that is grateful, a heart that is tender, a heart that is as open toward its world as is the heart of its Creator and Redeemer.

A Postscript: My brother Jack was two months dying with a brain tumor. He was the father of nine. During that period, his children came in from short and great distances, gathering around him, their mother, and one another. I discovered a few days after the burial that there had been some family division, rifts—two daughters hadn't spoken for six years, probably over something "worldly." The gathering, the dying and the death brought resurrection—the reconciliation of *all* divisions.

> *"Every worthwhile gift, every genuine benefit comes from God."*

AT THIS TIME

"My command to you is: love your enemies…"
—Matthew 5:38–48

Lord, the sun sets
on me,
and nobody dares
rain on my parade.

And I'll love
only Anglo-Americans,

not the "others,"
who are my enemies.

As for murderers,
rapists, and thieves,
I say, "kill them,"
incinerate them.

What's that, Lord?
You say your parade
was rained on
by civil servants?

What's that, Lord?
You say that you
were among
the alienated "others"?

What's that, Lord?
You say that you
were subject to
capital punishment?

COMPASSION BEARING FRUIT

Isaiah 55:1–3; Romans 8:35,37–39; Matthew 14:13–21

A newspaper photographer was sent to Ecuador in 1987 to cover the earthquake that devastated much of the country. In the midst of such catastrophic suffering, he witnessed a simple scene of compassion that moved him deeply.

The photographer wrote:

> The line was long but moving briskly. And in that line, at the very end, stood a young girl about 12 years of age. She waited patiently as those at the front of that long line received a little rice, some canned goods or a little fruit. Slowly but surely she was getting closer to the front of that line, closer to the food. From time to time she would glance across the street. She did not notice the growing concern on the faces of those distributing the food. The food was running out. Their anxiety began to show, but she did not notice. Her attention seemed always to focus on three figures under the trees across the street. At long last she stepped forward to get her food. But the only thing left was the lonely banana. The workers were almost ashamed to tell her that was all that was left. She did not seem to mind to get that solitary banana. Quietly she took the precious gift and ran across the street where three small children waited—perhaps her sisters and a brother. Very deliberately she peeled the banana and very carefully divided the banana into three equal parts. Placing the precious food into the eager hands of those three younger ones—one for you, one for you, one for you. She then sat down and licked the inside of that banana peel. In that moment I swear I saw the face of God!
>
> —JOHN JACKSON, *INDIANAPOLIS STAR*

What does it mean to be compassionate? One theologian says, "Compassion is the sometimes fatal capacity for feeling what it is like to live inside somebody else's skin…the knowledge that there can never

Chapter 10 • Compassion

really be any peace and joy for me until there is peace and joy finally for you too" (Frederick Buechner). Compassion is a response to suffering and an inward disposition that drives the ministry of Jesus. The Hebrew word for compassion has the same root as the word for womb. The womb protects and nourishes but does not possess and control. It yields its treasure in order that wholeness and well-being may happen. It is the way of compassion. To be moved with compassion then, involves a deep physical and emotional feeling. When the evangelists write about Jesus' compassion, it is this intensity of emotion that they are describing. Examples abound. "He was moved with compassion for the crowds," Matthew tells us. Jesus had compassion for the widow whose son had died. He was moved to compassion for the leper, the two blind men, and for his friend Lazarus.

> "COMPASSION IS THE CAPACITY FOR FEELING WHAT IT IS LIKE TO LIVE INSIDE SOMEBODY ELSE'S SKIN."

Jesus had been hungry himself. He knew what it meant to go without food. While he knew it wasn't the ultimate thing in life; he knew he couldn't get very far without it. Satan knew this as well and taunted Jesus to prove his divinity by turning most of the ground cover into enriched Wonder bread. There Jesus refused to flash his divine "union card" because performing miracles for the sake of the miraculous is not the way of God. But let the motivation for multiplying food be *compassion*, and Jesus confects an unparalleled feast that feeds a whole ball park.

The feeding of the five thousand serves as an example for all Christian ministry. More than just an enormous picnic happened in the minds and hearts of the people there by the Sea of Galilee. Something at the very heart and soul of the Christian faith was disclosed. That was the "economics of Jesus." Neither Karl Marx nor Milton Friedman would endorse it, but here it is:

> WHATEVER WE HAVE, NO MATTER HOW SMALL, HAS POTENTIAL WHEN PLACED IN THE HANDS OF GOD.

Whatever we have, no matter how small, has potential when placed in the hands of God, to grow beyond any humanly defined limits.

Notice Jesus does exactly what the disciples do not do: He doesn't fret or moan or despair over just having "five loaves and two fish." He simply says, "Bring them here to me." What the disciples consider inconsequential in light of so great a need, Jesus wants brought to him. What is the first thing he does? He lifts them to heaven and gives thanks, of all things. He doesn't ask God why there isn't more or complain about "insufficient resources." He exalts that which appears to be nothing.

Millard Fuller, founder of Habitat for Humanity, a ministry that builds homes *with* the poor, remarks that "Habitat is founded on the economics of Jesus, which was manifested in the feeding of the multitude." "Here it is," says Mr. Fuller, "you take what you have—even one dollar—and you give thanks for it and then give it to the Lord to be blessed. Then you step out in faith. Pagans need money in the bank before they start something. Not Christians. You take the first step, create a crisis where people know there is a poor family without shelter—motivated Christians will respond. God will provide."

Divine creativity is limited only by our capacity to accept it, to trust it and to be willing instruments of its unfolding. Such is the heart and soul of faith:

Compassion bearing fruit.

AT THIS TIME

"…for God is love."
—1 John 4:7–10

God's love
is unconditional:
we are loved
not merely in our doing
but in our *being*.

If we love others
unconditionally:
simply because they *are*,
we will know
the First Lover, God.

WATCH WITH BOTH EYES
John 9:1–41

According to Norse legend, the god Thor was responsible for protecting the world from the monsters of chaos. Every year he would make the complete circle around the globe, all the while beating back the monsters.

But every year Thor's orbit shrank. The protected circle became smaller and smaller. The god Thor had grown old and was weakening. Humankind was in danger. Chaos and hatred threatened to overwhelm order and peace.

The wisdom god, Woden, wondered what to do. Woden finally decided to confront the monsters of chaos. The wisdom god left the safety of his own circle and sought out the king of monsters. Woden and the monster king fought until Woden managed to overcome him. Bending the monster's arm back mercilessly, Woden demanded to know how order can be drawn out of chaos. "What is the secret?" Woden wanted to know.

"Give me your left eye," the monster king replied.

Woden immediately surrendered his left eye. "Now tell me."

The monster king smiled. "The secret is, watch with both *eyes."*

—JOHN GARDINER

Chapter 10 • Compassion

The question is, are we one-eyed people? The institution to me has been one-eyed for the past 400 years—one eye on ourselves and a jaundiced eye looking over our shoulders at those Protestants. It is only 100 years ago that one of our popes wrote about the Church in the modern world. Do we see only with the eye of practicality, self-interest and profitability? How often do we look through the eye of selfishness and humble faith? Do we see the eyes of faith beyond appearances and beyond superficialities, and look deeper to discover the timeless and profound truths that lie in the human heart?

As we look around the world, we recognize that the brokenness of the human condition haunts us like a recurring nightmare—bombing in New York City, craziness in Waco, drive-by shootings everywhere, insanity in Yugoslavia. Hope seems intermittent and fleeting. Where can we find wholeness in the world? Where to find light within the darkness of chaos? According to John's account of the healing of the blind man, we find it *in the streets*. Our healing does not come from retreat. Jesus and the blind man do not meet in the temple or synagogue. Their paths cross because they are "in the world" together. Parenthetically, John's Gospel, while the most mystical, the most imaginative of the Gospels, is also the most incarnational, the most earthy. (Sitting on the ground and making a paste and slapping it on the kid's eyes—pretty earthy.) Though they met in the streets, we know, of course, that Jesus spent much of his time in prayer alone in the desert, or in a quiet place, away from the din of the world, discerning his Father's way for him… *in the world*. The man born blind—in his very poverty of sight—was most likely prayerfully open, on tip toe, hopeful of healing. But they met "in the street."

As with all of Jesus' signs in the Gospel of John, this one symbolizes the fact that the whole world *is* reconciled to God by Jesus' life, death and resurrection. Nothing changes that; nothing can finally prevail against this reconciling act of God.

> I FIND CONVERSION AND CHANGE HAPPENING AMONG THE MOST *UNLIKELY* PEOPLE.

Yet the world as we know it is, has been, and will be good, bad, and every conceivable degree in between. As we journey in the world, believing in Jesus' Word and the Kingdom's presence, we watch with *both* eyes, with the *limited* vision of the human condition, the world's conventional wisdom, and with the *unlimited* vision of Christ's way, truth and life. Lent is our annual reminder of this vision and journey.

John's report of the blind man's healing and the reactions of the Pharisees to what Jesus has done, also reveals how unlikely people bear witness to the peace-filled presence of God's reign. What is more unlikely than the woman at the well last week—this blind man today, or Lazarus next week? John is clear: sometimes the world is receptive (the blind man); sometimes the world is hostile (the Pharisees). Yet, when God is present, the likely and the unlikely find themselves in surprising relationships of revelation, if we have eyes to see and ears to hear. When I look back on my years as a priest, I find conversion and change happening among the most *unlikely* people.

The world is not a passive recipient of God's presence and power. The incarnation and the sacramental realities of the Christian life tell us that the world itself can express the kind of life to which the gospel calls us. It does for instance in the words of a song called "The Rose."

> It's the heart afraid of breaking
> that never learns to dance.
> It's the dream afraid of waking
> that never takes a chance.
> It's the one who won't be taken
> that cannot seem to give.
> And the soul afraid of dying
> that never learns to live.

Perhaps this world will seem no better or worse because of our witness. I believe that in our openness to the call of the gospel we will discover that we too heal the sick, cleanse lepers, cast out demons and raise the dead. I've experienced people sick of heart become themselves again in the faith. I've witnessed AIDS victims find inclusion, not exclusion, in faith communities. I've known persons consumed by anger and hatred become forgivers. We've all known persons dead through various addictions come to life again—maybe because we've been there for them, or somebody has. I could walk through this community this morning and touch people who have been changed by this community, who have grown because of it and who are happier because of it. We are all healers, and it restores us to life.

To see the world with the vision of faith empowers us to recreate our world, empowers us to illuminate the darkness of oppression and violence with the light of compassion and justice.

"The secret is, watch with *both* eyes."

Chapter 11

PRAYER

ON RETREAT

Revelation 22:20

"Come, Lord Jesus!"
(to quote the prayer
of my heart)

knowing full well
that he is
already there

(has always been)

waiting
for me
to be,

saying:
"Come, William!"

and I
hesitantly reply:
"Yes, I am coming soon!"

Amen!

"Come, Lord Jesus!"

GOD'S LOVE

John 3:16–18

It is not often that a biblical verse is flashed across the television screens of America—especially when the event covered is not considered religious. Yet, it seems behind the goal posts and every place kick in the NFL, or in the stands during the World Series, a cardboard sign raises aloft "John 3:16," our reading for today: "God so loved the world that He gave His only son, that whoever believes in him may not die but may have eternal life." In the midst of all the uproar and tension of an athletic event, these cardboard signs stand out in stark, fundamentalist fervor. A silent code jostles for space amid the frenzied vision of modern sports: John 3:16.

Love: a word used so lightly, so loosely today. And yet the whole of the Christian life rests on this word "love," summarized in two verses from another text: "As the Father loved me I also have loved you; as I have loved you so also you must love one another." We might first explore what this text of John 3:16 does *not* mean. It does not mean that God saved Jesus from suffering, from temptation, from human limitation or loneliness. Jesus was not preserved from being misunderstood, rejected or humiliated, or from what the world called "failure." Jesus was not even saved from the experience of feeling abandoned by God or the experience of death.

What then does the Scripture reveal about the meaning of God's love for Jesus? Abba shared presence and power, life and love, or we might say, God's *all* with Jesus. "The One who sent me is with me." Jesus lived *out of* that truth. The praise or blame by others did not define Jesus. The success of his work did not give his life meaning. He believed that he was Beloved of God, and it is that truth that freed him up to be Jesus! It freed him up to eat with sinners, touch lepers and befriend women. He was free to disregard meaningless regulations and free to challenge self-righteous religious leaders. It made him free to cry over a city that did not know the things that were needed for its peace. His security in Abba's love freed him to acknowledge his fear of suffering at Gethsemane and his need for friends to be with him. It also freed him to go to his death, a seemingly senseless, brutal death.

GOD'S LOVE FOR US IN JESUS DOES NOT MEAN THAT WE WILL BE SAVED FROM SUFFERING.

God's love for *us* in Jesus does not mean that we will be saved from suffering, from human limitations, from loneliness; it does not mean that we will be preserved from misunderstanding, rejection, humiliation or what the world calls "failure." We may not even be saved from the experience of a sense of abandonment by the Lord, and certainly not from the experience of death.

What *does* Scripture reveal about Jesus' love for us? Well, Jesus, through the Spirit, has shared the mystery of his presence and his power with all who believe; that is, his life and love, or we might say, his *all*. "I call you my friends; I will be with you always; I have come that you may have life to the full."

It is clear that Jesus had a generous heart, a heart that was stretched to hold the very love of God in it; therefore he had a similar capacity for pain. Jesus had the kind of heart that agonized with the suffering of a paralyzed man, a stooped woman, a blind person. His heart ached over those in moral bondage, longing to set them free: the woman caught in adultery, Zacchaeus in his rich poverty, the religious leaders in their blind arrogance. Jesus' love persisted in spite of his friends' blunders and betrayals.

We were saved *not* by the physical death of Jesus, but by the absoluteness of a love that did not count death too high a price. It is *not* a love *for* suffering that Christ reveals, but a love that prevails *in* suffering. As Jesus was sent to be a sacrament of God's love for the world, we are called in faith to be sacraments of Jesus' love, in our love for one another:

- to heal
- to nourish
- to strengthen
- to forgive and
- to challenge

It is when we *believe* in God's personal love for each of us that we can be freed to love others.

Thomas Aquinas said somewhere: "God cannot love us more in eternity than He does at this very moment; God cannot love us less, no matter what, for He loves us infinitely." Ordinarily, most of us have no problem saying that to one another and firmly believing it, whether it is to the homeless person, the unwed mother or the one on drugs. We can say it to the dying cancer patient, to the little one, to the elderly; but often, we find it so hard to say it to ourselves and *believe* it. God had to remind Moses, "The Lord, the Lord, a merciful and gracious God, slow to anger and rich in kindness and fidelity."

THE MEDDLER

John 14:15–21

"The Father will give you," Jesus tells us, "the Spirit of truth, whom the world cannot accept since it neither sees nor recognizes the Spirit." The biblical command to love can be translated, "Love your neighbor; he or she is like you." This bypasses the question of self-love and focuses on equality. There are three essential elements of this love: giving and taking, attentiveness and pain.

Giving and taking stresses the *relational* quality of love; the concept "love of others" denotes a *relationship between people* and not the virtue of any single person. The basis of equality, then, is all of us have to *give*, and all of us have to *receive*. If I cease to take and give, I become a stone. So instead of saying, "It is better to give than to receive," we should say, "It is more blessed to give *and* receive than to have and hold." If my hands are fully occupied in holding on to something, I can neither give nor receive.

Chapter 11 • Prayer

In order to learn this kind of mutuality we need to develop *attentiveness*. When we talk about learning to love, what we really have to learn is to attend to the reality of the other person. We are *in*attentive to the reality of others the instant we regard them from the standpoint of their utility to us.

The third element, pain, results from the other two: the more attentive we become, the more we are open to giving and taking, the more vulnerable we become to pain. In Christian terms pain is inseparable from love. Jesus wept over the city of Jerusalem. That we always remain *behind* love, can never catch up with it, is the definition of messianic pain in an unredeemed world.

In our industrial society, love has been banished from public life. The rules that hold in a family and are taught in catechism do not apply outside the familial realm. Love your neighbor but not in public.

For historical reasons, American Catholic Christians have a tendency to regard "religion" as relevant to our *personal* lives but not to the *structures* of society. I remember some years ago a religious educator from the South stated that, where she came from, if a preacher talked about social or political issues, the congregation said, "He's quit preachin' and gone to meddlin'." So, I've "gone to meddlin'." I have been a meddler for thirty-three

> I HAVE BEEN A MEDDLER FOR THIRTY-THREE YEARS. PUT ON MY TOMBSTONE "THE MEDDLER."

years. Put on my tombstone "The Meddler." Love that we define as the capacity to seek out others *for their own sake*, and not for any *use* they can be to us, has become restricted to the private sphere. The economic, political and technical spheres of human life are regulated by quite different laws and sanctions— by the world that does not recognize the Spirit of truth.

This reduction of love to the private sphere of the family has resulted in further diminishment of love everywhere. In the long run what has become *objectively* impossible, meaningless and empty in society cannot be maintained *subjectively*; and the attempt to put the values we orient our life around into two separate compartments has failed. In a world that recognizes no other objects than those that are utilitarian or that satisfy desires, in a world that has reduced the range of human activities to nothing but production and consumption, in a world in which giving and taking have been reduced to buying and selling, the attentiveness of love cannot even emerge much less grow. One of our more enlightened corporations refers to employees likely to be laid off as "surplus." How would you like to be called "surplus"?

> THE SPIRIT OF TRUTH MAY VERY WELL BE WITH US BUT EVIDENTLY THE WORLD CANNOT SEE HIM.

In this crisis situation in which love has been reduced to a private, powerless and sentimental affair, it would seem that newer and better designs for human life are essential. The Spirit of truth may very well be with us but evidently the world cannot see nor recognize this Spirit. The technological solution says, "What human beings need is not love; their needs are as subject to planning and manipulation as anything else." The Gospel would suggest that love is perhaps the deepest need that we have, learning to give and to receive our greatest task. What is threatened now is *awareness* of this need, the very fact of its existence. Is the technocratic solution, which declares our deepest needs unreal and tries to manipulate them out of existence, the only solution? Or can we conceive of a society that takes these needs more seriously than all past ages have, because it seeks to establish giving *and* taking on a different economic basis for *all* people?

> Much advance publicity was made for the address the Master would deliver on the subject "The Destruction of the World," and a large crowd gathered at the monastery grounds to hear him. The address was over in less than a minute. All he said was:
> "These things will destroy the human race:
> politics without principle,
> progress without compassion,
> wealth without work,
> learning without silence,
> religion without fearlessness
> and worship without awareness."
>
> —Anthony de Mello

AT THIS TIME

"Dismiss all anxiety from your minds."
—Philippians 4:6–9

If, in Christ Jesus,
I present my needs
    to God in prayer
    and gratitude,
then God's own peace,
    even in turmoil
    even in grief
    even in uncertainty
    even in fear
will stand guard over
    my heart and mind.

FILL THE HEART WITH WONDER

Sirach 35:12–14,16–18; 2 Timothy 4:6–8,16–18; Luke 18:9–14

A monk was walking in the monastery grounds one day when he heard a bird sing. He listened, spellbound. It seemed to him that never before had he heard, really heard, the song of a bird. When the singing stopped he returned to the monastery and discovered to his dismay that he was a stranger to his fellow monks, and they to him. It was only gradually that they and he discovered that he was returning after centuries. Because his listening was total, time had stopped and he had slipped into eternity.

> Prayer is made perfect when the timeless is discovered. The timeless is discovered through clarity of perception.
>
> Perception is made clear when it is disengaged from preconception and from all consideration of personal loss or gain.
>
> Then the miraculous is seen and the heart is filled with wonder.
>
> —ANTHONY DE MELLO

With these two characters, the Pharisee and the sinner, we are given the two ends of the spectrum of the spiritual life. Both are a little absurd but the absurd is in the navel-gazing Pharisee, who presumes prayer is all about himself, not about getting out of his own way and truly giving thanks to God who is compassionate and merciful. I suspect that prayer is connected by many of us to the notion of *reward*, as Paul's waiting for God to "award" him his "merited crown" in the second reading. Putting the notion of *prayer* and *reward* too closely together can be a real problem in the Church, but evidently we have already been set up for it, in growing up Catholic.

The first issue, then, is whether prayer is best understood primarily as "requesting" things from God. In biblical terms, people did certainly pray to God to give them justice because human institutions had failed them. The presumption is that God actively and regularly intervenes in the world in place of human actors, or to countermand the evil work of others. This is, I would suspect, a naive assumption which Thomas Aquinas himself would have ruled out on two basic principles: one, the disproportion between God and human beings despite our "likeness" to God; and then, Saint Thomas' principle of secondary causality, which means that God "causes" things in this world, *not directly*, but in interaction with the free will and actions of others. Therefore, when I pray for justice, as Sirach in the first reading, I should not understand the object of the prayer to be that God will force other people to do things against their will so that "my will" is done. My prayer should be directed not at others at all, but principally that God so inspire *me*, that grace will interact with *my* free will, and I will act in the best way to establish justice—even when others refuse to act rightly.

What was right about the tax collector's prayer was not his abject humility, but his desire for mercy, for God's *presence* in transforming love. *Mercy* allows us not only to be forgiven whatever wrong *we* have done that might have contributed to the injustice we are presently suffering from, but to forgive—and even to act for the welfare of the oppressor.

Prayer, then, is not properly understood as being about "things," but about having the frame of mind, the "attitude," the "mind-set" of Jesus Christ—who is the *way*, the *truth* and the *life*. It is not wrong for an unemployed person to pray for work, or for a hungry person to pray for food, or a sick person to pray for health, as long as the prayer is always entered upon with the proviso that, come what may, God accompany us more closely *through* the difficulties of unemployment, hunger or sickness, and give us "what we need" *deep down*, even more than what we presume we know we need *up front*. Therefore the "reward" which the epistle calls the "merited crown" has nothing to do with laurel leaves (with which the victor's crown was made), or with "having" anything more. It was, rather, Paul's identification *with* Christ and the Kingdom. The only reward a Christian should pray for is God who *is* overwhelming *love*, God who is tender *mercy*, God who is graceful *Presence*, God who is utter *joy*.

> TO BE HOLY IS TO PUT ON THE MIND OF CHRIST, NOT CONVENTIONAL WISDOM.

The Jesus of Luke, earlier in the Gospel, says that if we seek and knock, God will give us the Holy Spirit—not things. Prayer for anything else is a distraction, even a form of idolatry. The same goes for intercessory prayer. Asking for things from patron saints, offering gifts to win a favor or get the saint's attention, is a problem. Have to be careful here. A few years ago a Catholic real estate broker in Tulsa said if you placed an upside-down statue of Saint Joseph in your front yard, you would sell your house. Wasn't that a wonderful witness to Jesus! That's what I call warmed-over paganism.

Intercessory prayer may not do much harm but it often distracts us from the task of becoming holy and replaces it with becoming satisfied (filled up)—

answered! To be holy does not mean some monk with head bowed reading his breviary with light coming in from the stained glass window. To be holy is to put on the mind of Christ, not conventional wisdom; to put on the mind of Christ in our real lives politically, socially and economically where we are in the world.

The prayer of the lowly and the publican "work" because they know "*their need for God,*" which is precisely what being "poor in spirit" means. They are not deluded by what they possess, or how smart they are to think that any endowment or "thing" can substitute for God's presence, God's love and God's mercy —which is timeless and, hopefully, filled with wonder.

AT THIS TIME

"Let it be done to me…"
—Luke 1:26–38

Troubled Mary
fearful virgin
wondering servant
favored daughter

emptied of self
now filled
with Presence:
Spirit's shadow
over you
incarnate Word
within you

let it be done to me
as it was with you.

Chapter 11 • Prayer

PRAY WHERE WE ARE

Mark 6:30–34

On a bitterly cold day a Rabbi and his disciples were huddled around a fire. One of the disciples, echoing his master's teaching, said, "On a freezing day like this I know exactly what to do!" "What?" asked the others. "Keep warm! And if that isn't possible, I still know what to do." "What?" "Freeze."

Present reality cannot be rejected or accepted. To run away from it is like running away from your feet. To accept it is like kissing your lips. All you need to do is see, understand, and be at rest.
—Anthony de Mello

In the game of cards called life, one plays the hand one is dealt to the best of one's ability…with God's help. Those who insist on playing, not the hand they were given, but the one they insist they should have been dealt—these are life's failures. We are not asked if we will play. That is not the option. Play we must. *The option is how.* Coming "to an out-of-the-way place," and resting a little is one of the ways Jesus taught them *how*. In our madcap society it is extremely difficult to rest. We have no time to reflect, no time to read, no time for serious reflection, no time to eat with leisure, no time to permit our spirit to expand—no time, if the truth were to be told, to live. (We hardly even have time to die.)

We rarely boast about our successes in reflecting, meditating, being silent, slowing down the pace of life. For these are not considered achievements. They don't prove our worth. Blue ribbons are for competition, not contemplation. G. K. Chesterton once wrote an essay on the importance of doing nothing. He argued that to do nothing was something very constructive and positive. Jesus and his friends, on occasion, had a little bit of time to do nothing on the shore of Galilee, even in the midst of an epochal change in human history: God taking flesh. Reflection, meditation, contemplation (whatever we call it) will help us embrace our option—and strive to become more fully what and who we are within family, occupations, relationships.

> FAR FROM BEING WORLD-FLEEING, OUR SPIRITUALITY WILL BE WORLD-SHAPING.

All of the ordinary things we do *have value in themselves*, and can express our love for God and neighbor, notably by the compassion and competence we bring to them; prayer time enables us to do this. We are obviously not monks or cloistered nuns. That is not the way we play (it is a valid way, but evidently, not ours). Our spirituality leads us to *stay* in the midst of the world and its structures and systems. Contemplation, a bit of silence, helps us to grasp "how" we stay in the world, helps us to ponder and realize that many of the structures and institutions that constitute our world are unjust, or otherwise out of harmony with gospel values, and "how" *we* exercise our role in the world. Far from being world-fleeing, our spirituality will be world-shaping, calling the structures and systems to change—including the church. Moments of prayer throughout the day—spontaneous turnings of our spirits to God—are a time-honored mode of prayer that fits in almost anytime or anywhere.

Catholic philosopher Jacques Maritan speaks of "the danger of seeking fullness *only* in the desert… and the danger of forgetting the necessity of the desert for fullness." A paradox: while the fullness of the Christian life is not restricted to the desert, still every full Christian life has need of some desert, some space, solitude, quiet time for prayer. These are momentary interludes to nourish and strengthen a person who is called to seek the Lord in his or her everyday life…while walking the dog, jogging, or driving to work. Our spirituality—a secular spirituality—will, above all, urge a great freedom to pray as we can, not as we can't, and especially to pray *where* we are. In the final analysis each one is called to strike a balance in prayer that reflects the wisdom of the monks, and at the same time, recognizes the validity of the very different context of *being in the world*. Some commonplace traits of our spirituality can be summed up in simple guidelines: *Be* where we are; be *who* we are; shape the world where we are; share with others while doing it. *Pray* where we are.

A Maryknoll missioner tells this story:

> The piety of a small girl in the Mexican town where I was pastor was remarkable. Passing the church on her way to school each day, she would

drop in to visit the Blessed Sacrament. A local resident known for his attacks on the Church also noticed her. One day he waited for the tot and confronted her. "Why do you enter the church so often?" he asked. "To talk to God," she replied. "Does God speak to you?" he continued. "Yes, in my heart," she said. "How big is your God?" he asked. Her response: "My God is big enough to be everywhere and little enough to live in my heart."

—JOHN P. LOMASNEY, M.M.

Chapter 12

POVERTY

SOLEMNITY OF CHRIST THE KING

Christ the King:

born in a stable
no MasterCard here

born sceptered
in weakness
simplicity his staff

born out of poverty
his family his wealth

born crowned with straw
only animals applaud

born into servanthood
not to be served

born in a manger
a powerless child

born swaddled in cloth
prefiguring his shroud

born to be light
while darkness prevailed

born in silence
below angel's song

born favored of God
favored not by his own

born among kings
like Herod the fox

born blessed by Simeon
contradiction's clue.

Christ the King:

lived without a place
to place his head

lived as a servant
his subjects his lords

the ruler of rulers
on his knees washing feet

lived among fisher folk
humanity his catch

lived eating and drinking
with social riff-raff

lived doubting
and debating
the conventional wisdom

lived often ignoring
his religion's laws

lived with rejection
from the elders of the land

lived with good news
his word unheard

lived with frustration
for the twelve
he had chosen

lived amid paradox
parables proclaimed:

having by giving
finding by losing

living by dying
gaining by denying.

Christ the King:

Tried through betrayal
by one of the twelve

a kangaroo court
of kings and fools

stripped of his clothes
now dressed in purple

coronetted with thorns
now a reed
for a scepter

mocked and spat upon
"hail, king of the Jews!"

Christ the King:

died criminally indicted
hung among thieves

died enthroned on wood
capitally punished

died seemingly forsaken
his friends on the lam

died hungry and thirsty
quenched with cheap wine

died and ill-welcomed
a stranger among his own

died dressed in humanity
imprisoned alone

died alive
when he could have
died dead

died as a king
a crucified scandal

died to be buried in a
borrowed tomb.

Christ the King:

Risen and present
though a stranger still

a gardener to Mary
to Peter a cook

bread blessed and broken
the least among us

still hungry and thirsty
still naked and estranged

still ill and imprisoned
still homeless and forsaken

when we do it for them
we do it for him

Christ the King.

SERIOUS ANOINTING

Isaiah 11:1–10; Romans 15:4–9; Matthew 3:1–12

The young disciple was such a prodigy that scholars from everywhere sought his advice and marveled at his learning.

When the governor was looking for an advisor, he came to the Master and said, "Tell me, is it true that the young man knows as much as they say he does?"

"Truth to tell," said the Master with irony, "the fellow reads too much. I don't see how he could ever find time to know anything."

—Anthony de Mello

If I suddenly called you a nest of hornets or a collection of poisonous snakes, you probably wouldn't be here next week, and there would be a movement to remove me. There may still be. But look what John the Baptist is doing —called the people who come to him a "brood of vipers." They are coming to be baptized, just as we come to church to worship, to sacraments. Shouldn't John encourage them for taking the right step? That's not enough for John, not until they "give some evidence—hard facts—that they mean repenting to reform"—willing to change. This could be a reminder to us that coming to church is not enough. The rituals are not enough. The sacraments we celebrate say "go further." To read Scripture or hear it read or preached is not enough. The Word has to move us, change us, not just inform us—as the "young disciple" in our story—and through us to change the world we live in. Too often we stop at a personal conversion, unaware or unwilling to think about the structures and systems of our society. Today, personal conversion is not enough.

Today, we live in a global village. Today, Guatemala is not a distant country, but next door. The entire world is growing apart into the haves and the have-nots, the people with too much to eat and the people who have nothing to eat at all. We are told, of course, that it will always be that way so we can sit on our hands and await the advent of the Kingdom, when Jesus comes on the clouds of heaven in power and glory! Let me suggest, and it may be a bit heretical, that there will be *no* Kingdom coming unless *we* prepare a place for it. To deny that we are collaborators is to deny the incarnation. We are the Christ of our time called to shape the world. So what is the function of Holy Mother Church, to save souls, in a world of massive oppression, dehumanizing poverty, hunger and exploitation...a world still threatened by nuclear and ecological disaster?

The role of the church—let me share with you a case history of a bishop in America, who, in all likelihood, should never have done what he did: he became a prophet. Here was this white Anglo bishop, John Fitzpatrick, from Florida, sent to work in the Hispanic diocese of Brownsville, Texas. Recently retired, because of age, he looks back on his ministry and I quote: "The Lower Rio Grande Valley is characterized by rapid population growth but only slow economic development. The Valley is among the poorest, most underdeveloped regions in the United States. There are twice as many families below the Federal poverty level as elsewhere in the nation. Unemployment tops 40 percent in some areas. The average wage is the minimum wage. The valley is in many ways an economic colony."

But this is not just a local problem, as we have indicated. He adds this metaphor: "The Valley is on what you might call an enormous fault line separating the two cities of a divided humanity, the city of the haves in the first world to the north and of the have-nots in the third world to the south. We see ourselves as something of a microcosm of the world, a world in collision with itself struggling to become one." If that is the scenario, what is the solution? The bishop again: "We could see that the extremes of poverty around us were accepted as an unfortunate but inescapable reality of life, as were the notions that women should remain in subordinate social roles, and that society can never really be healed of racial and other hatreds. These evils are unacceptable. So we resolved that issues of justice and the option for the poor would be at the *center* of all our ministry. How does this translate into action? Experience, not theory, is primary. Unless we change people's daily experiences from, say, being abandoned to being included, from being nobodies to being children of God, from possessing no dignity to possessing priceless worth, then we, as the church of Brownsville, would be on the way to nowhere."

That's not equal to the harsh language of John the Baptist, but it is a wake-up call. What did they do?

Chapter 12 • Poverty

The bishop and his co-workers established a refugee center, Casa Oscar Romero, where they sheltered, over a period of time, 130,000 people, and served over a quarter of a million meals. It became a storm center apparently over the issue of illegal aliens, but the bishop says pointedly (probably over and against the U.S. Naturalization Service), "We know a refugee when we see one; we know refugee rights. So do the United Nations and Amnesty International."

There is much more, such as job training, the energizing of lay people to take over programs, and, in general, a movement to reform —social reform, from the bottom up. This is a remarkable bishop and one could profoundly wish that his tribe increase.

> WE MUST DO MORE THAN WAVE OUR BAPTISMAL CERTIFICATES AT ST. PETER.

In the great Isaiah passage today we are told that the anointed One "will decide aright for the afflicted of the land." The anointed One *is* Jesus Christ, but *so are we*; we are all anointed. Bishop Fitzpatrick and his co-workers took that anointing seriously, as many do in this parish. (Parenthetically, a good Catholic high school in Tulsa is building a four million dollar *athletic* complex with private funds—and nobody questions it. I have to wonder at times if the diocese of eastern Oklahoma is on its way to nowhere. Now, having said that, I may be on my way.) The angry prophet called John warns us, we must do more than wave our baptismal certificates at St. Peter. Perhaps we begin by "accepting and welcoming one another as Christ has accepted you," in the words of Paul. And then, in various ways, support or engage in projects of social issues. People who do this have not just received a baptism of water, but one of spirit—and of fire.

POVERTY

Poverty is darkness;
  not the dumb, dull darkness
    of not having
    the light
    of color television;
  not the damp, dreary darkness
    of not having
    brightly burning logs
    in the fireplace;
  not the dazzling darkness
    of not having
    a super-chromed V-8
    from Detroit.

Poverty is darkness;
  the devastating darkness
    of not having, period;
  not even having
    a simple shelter
    wherein to sleep my body;

not sufficient sustenance
>to enliven my flesh,
not a simple shirt or dress
>to hang on my back
>or breast.

Poverty is darkness;
>the darkness of despair
>>for the lack of
>>self-determination;
>the darkness of being powerless
>>in the midst of many powers.

And, in a nation,
>parenthetically "under God,"
>>poverty is pornographic.

DAN'S WEALTH

Ecclesiastes 1:2; 2:21–23; Luke 12:13–21

I would like to share with you a friend's dream, but first, some background. A community of sisters, the Incarnate Word, operates St. Francis Hospital in Tulsa. Every year this community, based in Houston, gives a grant of $20,000 to Neighbor for Neighbor, an anti-poverty movement in North Tulsa. I say "movement" because it is neither an agency nor an organization, and after twenty-five years has barely become institutional. NFN provides immediate services to the real poor of

Tulsa, most of whom, I would say, make less than $5,000 to $6,000 per year. There are five medical clinics each week; two optometric clinics; two dental clinics; a legal clinic, which in six months of service has resolved over 400 cases for people who have had *no* access to the courts; a front office facility that responds to emergency needs; plus a grocery store in which only the poor can shop. In addition to immediate services, the movement called Neighbor for Neighbor is political, taking on giants like the utilities, the Corporation Commission, housing authorities, and real estate brokers, always in behalf of the poor. The fiscal year ending August 30, they will have responded to over 30,000 individual cases. Their budget is now $500,000—receiving funds neither from United Way nor the Federal Government. By the way, this is not a fundraising address. I don't raise funds for anybody too well.

A few weeks ago, the Incarnate Word sisters invited NFN's Director, Dan Allen, to meet with them in relation to the yearly grant. There is no adequate way to describe Dan Allen, my closest friend, who was a priest when he began NFN 25 years ago. Dan, now in his early sixties, is an irascible yet compassionate curmudgeon with a sense of humor, who has managed, in a real prophetic way, to put together a most remarkable community of diverse people who work directly *with* and *for* the poor. The sisters asked Dan and all their grant recipients to present a one-page *"dream paper on solving poverty."* In view of the reading today I would like to share with you Dan Allen's dream, the one-pager he sent to the good sisters:

Chapter 12 • Poverty

I believe poverty begins when income decreases or ceases. The protection and utilization of what income there is, is paramount.

Beyond what already exists at Neighbor for Neighbor, I would put into place a major financial institution that was tailored *to* and administered *by* low- and no-income people...for today's banks, mortgage firms, and savings and loan institutions simply do not qualify to serve poor people. The poor are forced to either lose all they have or pay exorbitant interest or become wards of the government.

Concomitant with loss of income is the loss of self-worth and all that entails. To combat this, the New Testament calls for believers to live by the *New* Law, which, of course, is the Beatitudes from Matthew's Sermon on the Mount. Since this is why religious institutions and churches are tax-free, I would lobby for state and federal laws which would tax religious institutions that do *not* live by the New Law—and the proceeds would go to the aforementioned financial institutions set in place to serve the poor.

Finally, in this dream, I would like to be the Pope for seven days. I would replace the Code of Canon Law with the Beatitudes as being the only law, not only for the people but also for the institutional church to live by. I would decree the absolute right of freedom of conscience for all people. I would prohibit all new ecclesiastical construction, and would replace the entire College of Cardinals with women so that the Church might reclaim her soul.

Then, I believe, poverty would fade because the glory of God would then be *all* people fully alive.

The rich man in today's gospel has much concern for his wealth but it's all directed toward his own well-being. And God asks him: "To whom will all this piled-up wealth of yours go?"

Dan Allen is the Ecclesiastes man "who has labored with wisdom and knowledge and skill," and will leave behind him a legacy of wealth far greater than the wealth of all the affluent in our society.

"To whom," God asks us, *"will all this piled-up wealth of yours go?"*

THE MAKING OF A KING

Once upon a time, there lived a people who, after centuries of democracy, demanded a king to rule over them.

The very local god, called Gnp for short, had inspired the Amoral Amajority to place economics at the center of the citizen's lives. Gnp's commandments were two: Love money above all things, with all your heart, mind and soul. The second was like the first: Love yourself the more you have of it.

A king was desperately needed…a king to rule absolutely. After all, some lackluster legislature might vote to share the wealth, and that wouldn't do.

The first regent to reign was the personable orator and one-time thespian, Reginald Regal. Ol' Reggie had great faith in the Gnp and developed the national philosophy. Summed up, it went like this: Life begins at conception and ends at birth…ends,

Chapter 12 • Poverty

that is, for the poor and powerless. On the other hand, life begins for the rich and powerful, and evidently, never ends—an eternal cycle of acquisitions and garage sales, garage sales and acquisitions—reaching its full, avaricious crescendo at Christmas time, a season lasting for eleven months. In January, the whole nation, except the poor, took a vacation. They went south of course, for by that time, they had, between the multinationals and the marines, acquired South America. Eventually, so much stuff was amassed that the First Annual International Hedonist Garage Sale was held in the nation's capitol.

> OL' REGGIE REGAL'S SON WAS APTLY NAMED BUICK REGAL.

The national resource was no longer people, but things. You were what you owned. Eventually, children were named after objects rather than after other people. One child was patriotically named Bank America. Another was christened MasterCard. If a girl, she was called Visa. Ol' Reggie Regal's son was aptly named Buick Regal. The rich loved to name their boys Fleetwood, and the girls Mercedes. The head of Reggie's Department of Interior was Baron Wastelands.

Ol' Reggie, now living in the White Palace, ordered prayers to be said in the public schools to their god, Gnp. Unfortunately, there were no public schools. Following the Edict of Tuition Credits, religious schools of piety flourished like weeds in every state. The Director of Education was, of course, Sir Jerry Fellbad, ol' Reggie's court jester and chaplain.

Back in the 20th century, P.R. (Pre Reggie), there was a government agency called the War Department, later changed to the Department of Defense. Under Reggie, it became the Department of Peace. The new Premier for Peace was Sir Casper Skywalker, who had the responsibility of directing the coming Star Wars, a new, real-life film in which ol' Reggie was starring and gleefully looking forward to.

And so, in this nation under Gnp, where prosperity was the ultimate measure of happiness, the absolute sign of Gnp's love, the middle-class disappeared, leaving only two realities: the rich and the poor. The poor went without; the rich went with. The poor starved; the rich consumed and consumed. The nation died; not from without, but from within; not with a bang, but with a whimper.

WAKE UP!

*Jeremiah 33:14–16; 1 Thessalonians 3:12; 4:2;
Luke 21:25–28,34–36*

I shared an apocalypse Saturday morning at 1:00 a.m. Temporarily wearing the Chaplain's pager, I was called to the hospital emergency room and listened to three young people tell the story of their father, shot and killed while driving a cattle truck through Bartlesville, Two brothers, Danny, 23, and John, 11, and their sister Melinda, 16, witnessed a tragic *end time* in their young lives…a

Thanksgiving weekend with their Dad became an apocalypse. A man in a pick-up truck toyed with the big diesel on Highway 75 and wouldn't let them pass. The children's father flicked his bright lights on and off and blew the diesel horn. The man in the pick-up finally let them pass, then shot the trucker as he went by, leaving the daughter to grab the wheel as the father slumped in his seat, dead. Too bad I didn't have a member of the National Rifle Association with me as I tried to console those kids. An apocalypse!

When Mark wrote the first Gospel (a literary form that Mark invented), he anticipated an imminent end to the world. For Luke, writing later, the situation has been dramatically altered: the Temple has been destroyed and the end has not come. The Second Coming is now set in the distant future.

Why did Luke retain this apocalyptic residue? *First of all*, he has evidently decided to use the end-time symbols and metaphors to play upon the depths of hope and fear within his own community. Cosmic images like these speak directly to the insecurity of each person, and the language reminds the listener, at the unconscious level, of the reality of one's own mortality. *Secondly*, Luke uses this to exhort his community to remain steadfast within the present time of their days...and the many "end times" they might experience. To urge a community to pray constantly in light of what *may* come means that the very prayer life of the community includes the intrusion of the future into their lives. While the Lukan community remembered *out of the past*, they lived *out of the future*. They drew their energy from the viewpoint that dealing with the various burdens and troubles of the present had far-reaching effect. Indeed, in those very situations that were most distressing and unsettling (such as persecution), there was the possibility of recognizing the Divine Hand, the Spirit's Presence. How well does the Church read the "signs of the times" and what needs to be done for the future? Do we find that our prayer is open to the One who is still coming? Out of what do we live?

What we can understand is that such a world envisioned by Jesus, a world of justice and compassion (a world in which words like rich and poor are meaningless), never could co-exist with the kind of world he lived in and Luke lived in and we live in. Ours is a world governed by greed and hunger for power, and by cynical disregard for the needs of those unable to compete for the prizes, who become, then, merely tools to obtain more wealth and power (for example, multinational factories across the border in Mexico).

In Jesus' world—the world Jeremiah called the *fulfillment* of God's promise—there is no room for competitive, exploitative behavior, so Jesus knew the existing world would not tolerate his Kingdom's values, and he saw (as Luke interprets) the transition from one to the other in terms of turmoil, fear and destruction. This is well confirmed from our own apocalyptic history as a nation. When men and women have tried to *live out* the *way* preached by Jesus, they have aroused suspicion and hostility and persecution (for example, conscientious objectors to the Persian Gulf War).

Chapter 12 • Poverty

It would seem that the challenge of Advent is to allow the symbolic poetry of both the *cosmic crisis* (sun, moon, stars), and the *present coming* of Jesus to inform our moral imagination, and to inform our political will, so that we, as Christian believers, never rest content to let the world of conventional wisdom interpret reality simply as it wills (for instance, Magic Johnson: it's okay to be sexually active—just do it safely. Hogwash!).

The stuff of politics—then as now—easily becomes trite compromise with a morality of the least common denominator, and pure accommodation to "bottom-line" analyses (that is, cash flow). And even here, where we expect real accountability, most often we get lies—even from the Church.

> WHERE WE EXPECT REAL ACCOUNTABILITY, MOST OFTEN WE GET LIES—EVEN FROM THE CHURCH.

It is not enough to "remember the homeless" at Christmas time, and lead our lives for the rest of the year as if homelessness were a *natural* phenomenon, and not the result of financial and political decisions.

That is why the theme for Advent is "wake up," lest we be lulled by Christmas music into feeling warm and cozy and lying to ourselves about our broader responsibilities, for we are *named*, according to Jeremiah, "the lord of justice!" That's *who* we are! And down through Advent we need to consciously remember that we are the exiles—pilgrims; *we* are Jerusalem, wasted and waiting for restoration; *we* are John the Baptist, demanding justice; *we* are his audience, wondering what to do; *we* are Mary, pregnant with Christ; *we* are a voice crying in the wilderness; *we* are a word, a poem wanting to be expressed, wanting to become flesh—full of grace and truth.

AT THIS TIME

"…They had come to know Jesus in the breaking of the bread."
—Luke 24:35–48

As we recount
what has happened to us
on the road to the Kingdom,
we discover sadly
that we have "come to know Jesus"
in the breaking of the
   "dough";
since wealth and power
get the incense,
we should genuflect
before entering the banks,
or bow our heads
before reading the
Wall Street Journal.

CARING FOR THE HUMAN SPIRIT

Jeremiah 20:7–9; Romans 12:1,2; Matthew 16:21–27

> *Husband: "I'm going to work hard, and someday we are going to be rich."*
> *Wife: "We are already rich, dear, for we have each other. Someday maybe we'll have money."*
> —A<small>NTHONY DE</small> M<small>ELLO</small>

From time to time, magazines unveil their list of the most influential Americans. If we were to list the top ten most influential Catholics of this century, one who would be on the list is Dorothy Day, founder of the Catholic Worker Movement. Wherever she was or whatever she was doing, a concern for the working person outlined her life. The entirety of her life story reveals numerous situations in which we could imagine the words of Jeremiah on *her* lips. Jeremiah reveals his struggles with the power of God's word in his life, and the "derision and reproach" that was the response to his message. Dorothy Day, outspoken radical that she was, often incurred the wrath of the Catholic hierarchy in New York City. She, like Jeremiah, experienced being an object of laughter and mockery.

The sense of mystery surrounding religious commitment, and the temptation to avoid embarrassment by not letting it be known, is an experience with which many Christians can identify. How many of us listen to racial jokes or slurs and let them go by without comment or correction? It is never comfortable to be the holder of an unpopular opinion. If one's position is the result of religious beliefs or values, the discomfort may be one of the reasons so many argue that religion has no place in business or the world of work—as if faith could be compartmentalized or turned off or on. Some folks, for example, assert that Catholic education must educate its students into a disciplined sensitivity toward the suffering in the world. And yet, our Catholic universities and academic system have educated the children of the rich and powerful in Central America for years, and for years they have returned to places like Guatemala and El Salvador with *no* sensitivity for the poor at all. Zero!

> IT IS NEVER COMFORTABLE TO BE THE HOLDER OF AN UNPOPULAR OPINION.

Since the corporate world has become so savage, there is a growing movement to include ethics in business school curricula, and some have begun to focus on the value of spirituality in the work place. This means an attempt to replace the model of business and work as a machine with a model that recognizes the benefit to be derived from having an environment characterized by spirituality. By spirituality, we mean an energy that inspires a person to certain ends and purposes that go beyond *self* in a society that is centered on self. We are not talking about monks wandering down monastery corridors with bowed heads and folded hands. We are talking about lay spirituality *in the world*.

An observation has been made by social scientists that employees perform more creatively when they believe they are contributing to a purpose larger than themselves, when they have a cause. It would appear that most people have work that is *too* small for their spirits. The discrepancy between the significance of the cause and the depth of the human spirit may be even greater for a Christian who chooses to see his or her work *in the world* as related to the work of Christ and the Christian community. Like the Word of the Lord burning in Jeremiah's heart—or Dorothy Day's—an individual's spirit becomes like a fire imprisoned in the bones, as she or he grows weary of holding it in. It would seem there must be an integrity between the individual's identity as a Christian person and *what* gives meaning to one's working life. St. Paul admonishes us: "*Do not conform* yourselves to *this* age, but be transformed by the renewal of your mind, so that you may judge what is God's will and what is good, pleasing and whole."

The *goals* of a larger salary, title, an expense account, the "corner" office, are not wrong, but are they good enough? Is the workplace transformable? What is the future of a person who chooses to integrate *all* of life—including work—into his or her *faith* life? The gospel paradox points to an answer: "Whoever would save one's life will lose it, but whoever loses one's life for my sake will find it." It is likely, therefore, that managers and employees alike who strive to create an atmosphere that is healthy for the human spirit will risk being misunderstood and seen as less competitive and less appropriate for promotion.

If the goal is to gain the world, there is danger of failing. But if the cause goes beyond the self, and the integration of work into one's identity is the goal, then work will still be work, but it will be worth doing. When work has meaning, then the human spirit will be at peace.

BE A LAMP

Isaiah 58:7–10; 1 Corinthians 2:1–5; Matthew 5:13–16

Every day, for 30 years, a professor of art in New York City walked past the French Consulate. But then, one day when she strolled by, it was newly and brightly lit for an art exhibit. She noticed under the new lights a three-foot sculpture that had stood there for nearly a half century, unnoticed. She and several art historians agreed it was very likely an early Michelangelo.

The Word summons us to identify with a lamp, of all things. For a moment then, be a lamp; let's say, an old dusty lamp with oil and wick:

I am a lamp, a container of things consumable. I am still, static, shelved, of little use, until someone strikes a match and turns me on. I am not an absolute self-starter but a dependent being. I need and want contact; I need to be touched to become fully alive, to become bright and warm and enlightening. I cannot be so in isolation. Without that relationship or contact, without that spark, I remain cold, unseen, alone. But given such intervention, such friction, I become fire myself. My potential to make the environment gladsome and cheerful is drawn forth. As a lamp, I become a focal point of orientation and attraction; I draw others out of their darkness, prevent their stumbling and confusion. I become a point of departure as well; my radiant light falls upon so many things, reveals their features, their beauty. Things once unseen, unnoticed, unappreciated, become visible in all their detail.

Yet, in all this, being a point of attraction as well as departure, I am also consumed. As a lamp, there can be no light, no radiance, no warmth, unless I am consumed. Everything hinges on my being diminished ...the lessening of my self-preservation and self-containment. As a lamp, if I am determined to hold on to what I've got, I will suffer no loss and stand absolutely still in the world. If I refuse contact with this troubled world in order not to be "taken," then I shall remain intact, but cold, dark, still, unborn. Only if I let go of myself, and give up my importance, and become vulnerable to the fire of life... only if I let my seeming substance go up in smoke will I really know what wholeness is. Then only will I achieve this strange, paradoxical transformation.

The match that struck Paul was Jesus who alone brings the fullness of life and light. Paul let go of his own wisdom and ways, and became vulnerable: open to a new light, a new way and a new truth. Today's reading says he came in weakness and fear, and with much trepidation; and precisely in that state, he became strong, bold and courageous, a light to others through the "power of the Spirit." Paul let his substance go up in smoke in order to experience what wholeness really meant. Paul came to realize that only an empty lamp is fillable. If then, I die to myself; if I let myself be consumed in the service of others; if I let go of my self-importance and become vulnerable, open to the light which is Christ; then, Isaiah tells me, poetically, "that light shall rise for me in the darkness, and the gloom shall become for me like midday."

DREAM TALK

Isaiah 62:1–5; 1 Corinthians 12:4–11; John 2:1–12

Martin Luther King's Legacy: the "new wine" of hope

Martin saw the fury in his brother's eye,
sparked by flames of fiery crosses,
settling in black bones at the back of the bus,
simmering in black souls from years of pushing brooms,
masked, controlled, straining to be unleashed
like hounds from hell hungry for white blood.

Pouring the rage into the cup,
and mixing it with justice and right and fists unclenched,

Chapter 12 • Poverty

> *he offered it to his brothers, saying, "Can you drink?"*
>
> *Martin had a dream of burdens unbroken, souls unchained,*
> *sisters and brothers free for standing tall and stepping light.*
> —Fr. Gene Ulses, *St. Anthony Messenger*

While driving to Tulsa the other day, I switched on National Public Radio, and tuned in to Martin Luther King, Jr., giving his "Dream" talk. The words were taped, of course, because he was killed by a sniper's bullet in 1969. In the speech I heard, he said to an enormously enthusiastic crowd: "I have a dream. I have a dream that my four little children will one day live in a nation where they will not be judged according to the color of their skin, but by the content of their character. I have a dream that one day all people will sit at one table, eating and drinking together. I have a dream…" We can all, to some degree, fill in the rest of what Martin Luther King dreamed about.

Mary had that same dream in the gospel story of today, when she saw her son coming to that wedding feast. It is the same dream—that old and ever-new human dream. Mary's dream reflected back on her "Magnificat," her own fabled dream song: "God has shown the power of his arm, he has routed the proud of heart. He has pulled down princes from their thrones and exalted the lowly." And so Mary dreamed that her son would continue God's mercy toward the lowly, that he would serve as a sign of God's fidelity to his promises. When she saw her son arrive, she thought to herself: *Maybe this is the beginning of it all. Maybe it is today, that from here, from this feast, from this house, from this table…from this kitchen all will start. Maybe after today I will no longer say, "I have a dream." Maybe today all is going to change. Maybe today, the final wine is going to flow.*

But her son sat with some people Mary had never seen before (she even thought she spotted a tax collector), and Jesus took a glass, and he started to drink like all the others, happy and relaxed. Mary thought: *Should I try? Should I provoke? Should I suggest?* Then suddenly she heard from the kitchen (that is where such news is always heard first): "No wine! This is the last jug! What are we going to do?" There were too many guests, no wine, and no money, either.

> JESUS, RELUCTANTLY, GAVE HIS MOTHER AND FRIENDS A PREVIEW OF COMING ATTRACTIONS.

It was as if the sign had already been given; the old was over, the new should start. She decided and went to him and said, "They have no wine!" He looked at her and said, "Not yet, not yet!" But she went to the kitchen anyway and ordered, "Do whatever he tells you." This is what they did: after some time, Jesus stood up, went to the kitchen and told them to fill all the available pots and pans with water. They filled them up to the brim and all the water was changed into wine. And so Jesus, reluctantly, gave his mother and friends a preview of coming attractions, for he too had a dream, a dream where he saw himself fulfilling Isaiah's dream, "to bring glad tidings to the poor, to proclaim liberty to captives." John says that this was the first of the signs that would lead to his final work. Mary was right. She knew that the final banquet would start, but she did not know when. Her timing was bad, but she knew it would come: the time when the dream would no longer be a dream. The sign was given. He intervened in the work she told the others to do.

And his disciples believed in him.

One of those disciples, very many years later, was Martin Luther King, Jr. and again, like many, he said, "I have a dream..." That was not all he had. That was not all he did. He worked, desolate and forsaken, sweated and died filling the empty jugs of this world with water, believing that once again Jesus would come to change all that water, the bitter racist water of this world, into wine—sweet, good, grade A, heavenly wine, *preparing* for the banquet to come.

Perhaps it is time for us, who believe with Paul, that the Spirit has been given to us for the "common good"... time for us to enter the kitchen of this world —doing what he instructed us, through prayer and action—getting ourselves prepared for him who will do it with us, that is, bring the dream of fulfillment ... serving the choice wine *now!*

FAITH REALITIES FOR OUR TIME

Isaiah 61:1,2,10,11; 1 Thessalonians 5:16–24; John 6:1–8,19–28

Jesus, at the beginning of his public life, stood up in his hometown synagogue and delivered his inaugural address, quoting from today's first reading: "The Spirit of the Lord is upon me…" Later on in his public life, at one of his mountaintop press conferences, Jesus made a policy statement: "Blessed are the poor in spirit…those who mourn…those who are gentle…those who hunger and thirst for justice…" Finally, at the end of his public life, Jesus delivered his "State of the Kingdom" message. "For I was hungry and you gave me food, thirsty and you gave me drink…"

Let us, for a moment at least, pull our heads out of the sands of history and face faith realities for *our* time, for *today* is still Jesus' time. The Spirit of the Lord is upon *us* (not somebody else), because the Lord through sacrament has anointed us and through the sacrament called us Church—the body of Christ (that's us!). *We* are sent to bring glad tidings to the lowly (that's why the Sousas are taking 200-plus gifts from us to the children of Hayti, Missouri). *We* are sent to the brokenhearted (that's why we struggle to be present to the bereaved and grieving). *We* are sent to proclaim liberty and release to prisoners—not only the folks in jail (them too) but those held captive by illness, loneliness, poverty. *We* are sent to announce, by our lived lives, a year of *favor* (a better word for "grace") from the Lord to truly build a kinder, gentler nation *for all*, not just the powerful. And because of the faith that sends us—compels us—to fulfill the promises, we rejoice heartily in the Lord, "in our God is the joy of the soul"—not merely in ourselves.

It is God who has clothed us in Christ, who has helped us to put on the Lord. It is God who has wrapped us in a mantle of justice—covered us from head to toe with Christ's peace. We are like the bride or bridegroom bedecked, adorned with treasures—jewels of mercy, gentleness, patience, compassion.

> WE ARE SENT TO ANNOUNCE, BY OUR LIVED LIVES, A YEAR OF FAVOR FROM THE LORD.

And so Paul tells us "to rejoice always, never cease praying—render constant thanks, do not stifle the Spirit given to us." The gospel gathers Isaiah and Paul and the bug-eater John and ourselves into a grand summation. The gospel reads this way at *this* time:

There is a Community named St. James, sent by God to be witness to the light so that through it others might believe. We are not the light ourselves, but called to testify to the light, who is Christ. How often do we, as church, seem to testify to ourselves as the light? Or to our culture as the light? The testimony we give when the world comes to ask "Who are you?" is the absolute statement: "We are not the Messiah. We are not people overflowing with great

wisdom. We are not people of power. We are not even very good prophets." "Then," the world replies, "tell us who you are. What do you have to say for yourselves?"

And how do we answer? What *do* we have to say for ourselves? Can we say: "We are the Community of St. James, a voice in the desert crying out, 'Make straight the *way* of the Lord'"? Are we a voice of truth in the desert of greed and power, or are we ourselves careening down the wreck-strewn *way* of the world leaving in our path hunger and disease, destitution and despair? Or are we struggling to reflect the light of the Lord's *way*—the way of paradox: gathering by sharing, having by giving, living by dying, finding by losing, experiencing strength through weakness—because we believe in the Spirit of the One who is with us always, the strap of whose sandal we are not worthy to unfasten.

This is happening in Bartlesville, across the Caney, where Christ is present.

BEING A PASTORAL CHURCH

I stand here this morning rather humbled by the overwhelming witness to Christ reflected by last night's nominees for the

Chapter 12 • Poverty

Dorothy Day Justice Award, and by Velma Russell, the recipient of the award. This is the pastoral church working at its very best, the church of Veronica wiping the face of Christ's poor in the world. I want to share with you another model, one that we could call the prophetic model. If the good Samaritan on the road to Jericho had to stop *every* day to lift a man—beaten by robbers—out of a ditch, and care for him at the local Comfort Inn, I suppose he would soon begin to wonder about the *state* of the road, and perhaps act to change the conditions that made the road so dangerous for travelers.

Question: When will Americans accept full responsibility for public life as Catholics? In both our liberal and conservative variations, Christian assimilation *to* the *American way of life* has brought *accommodation* to public philosophies of declining substance and vigor. We have not impacted on our culture, our culture has impacted on us...seduced us. Our paralyzed politics (gridlock), brittle culture (it is to be noted that the most popular home to visit, second only to the White House, is Graceland), and mean-spirited public life can hardly attend to questions of the *common good:* the demands of justice that scream for redress and redistribution.

Indeed, the style of governance we have witnessed these past several years has not only ignored those cries, it has put at risk our very ability to provide the most basic necessities: personal security, housing, education and health care. We have, as American people, whatever our religious persuasion, relinquished basic norms—like the *social* nature of human beings; their rights and responsibilities within an attentive community; the reasonable discourse that governs and sustains such communities through vigorous politics. These are the very standards that the best of our Christian tradition espouses for civil society, yet our individualistic and avaricious society has hardened its hearts against these criteria of community and justice.

> REVELATION DEMANDS A COMPASSIONATE VISION.

The fact that there *is* sin in the world, that it is systemic, social, present and ubiquitous, is proved by our Pax Christi gathering this weekend. We have, if we include our Judaic tradition, more than 4,000 years of combined revelation telling us incessantly and clearly that there is in our collective wisdom a *preferential option* for the poor; any other option is *un*acceptable. Our revelation tells us that there is a call to retain a special openness with the small and the weak, those who suffer and weep, those who are humiliated and marginalized, so as to help them *own* their dignity as human persons and children of God; that there is imposed upon us by revelation and tradition a prophetic mandate to speak *for* them, to be a defender of the defenseless who, in biblical terms, *are* the poor; to be *for* and *with* them, and not, by washing our hands, turn them over to Pilate whether that be the government or United Way.

Revelation demands a compassionate vision that enables faith communities to see reality from the side of the poor, to assess our life-style as well as social institutions and policies in terms of their impact on the poor. *Item:* Recently in Tulsa, Oklahoma, the church closed down a parish school on the edge of the black community (which served the black community) for what we called "lack of funds." Within two years, four million dollars in Catholic money was quickly raised to build *athletic* facilities at our white diocesan high school.

I would suggest three basic moral principles or priorities to govern public policy when we have intergroup tensions to claim:

1. The *needs* of the poor take priority over the *wants* of the rich. (The school serving the black community should have priority over the athletic needs of the affluent white kids.)
2. The *freedom* of the dominated takes priority over the *liberty* of the powerful. (Apply that to NAFTA, the so-called Free Trade Agreement.)
3. The *participation* of the marginalized takes priority over the *preservation* of an order that excludes them. (To the banks, the poor do not exist; they are economic non-persons.)

The quest for justice is *never* a purely *secular* affair. It has its roots in the biblical tradition that continues in our day—to seek, to create, to make incarnate a dwelling place for God in our human history. And yet, quite sadly, another message is being clearly proclaimed in our land: churches and synagogues are to concern themselves with the private individual sins of their people...and not concern themselves with the social sin of the nation, thereby calling into question the institutional arrangements of the country. The Christian communities are free from government harassment so long as they proclaim a privatized and trivialized Word of God. We can believe anything we like as long as it does not have adverse repercussions on the current system—a system designed *by* the powerful *for* the powerful. I personally believe that people of *authentic biblical* faith and the American way are on a collision course.

Perhaps we seriously need to dream of life in different terms. From abundance as a symbol of God's blessings, to abundance as a resource for other's needs. From worship as an exercise of personal piety, to worship as a community's search to know God's will *in* the world, not in the chapel. From salvation as a strategy to increase attendance rolls, to salvation as a process of becoming one with God through our neighbor. From wealth as a just reward for sixty-hour weeks, to wealth as an impediment to the Kingdom. From power as a status to be sought, to power as an evil to be rejected. From liberation as a license to instant gratification, to liberation as a freedom from human-made economic, political and social barriers. From justice as a future hope for the *have-nots*, to justice as a goal to be initiated *now* by the *haves*.

Identification with the poor is *not* an option in our biblical tradition. It is rather the *core* of faithfulness—a lifetime of growing rich in the sight of God.

RESPONSE FORM

☐ Please send me information regarding any future works by Father Bill Skeehan.

_____
NAME

_____
ADDRESS

_____
CITY   STATE   ZIP

We welcome your comments regarding *To Dance With A Cross On Our Back*. Please use this opportunity to share with us how you used the book, what it meant to you, personal stories, etc. Some comments may be used in future volumes by Father Skeehan, unless otherwise requested.

_____

_____

_____

_____

_____

_____

_____

_____

Complete this form and mail in an envelope to:
> Father Bill Skeehan
> The Community of St. James
> 5500 Douglas Lane
> Bartlesville, OK 74006